A gift to you with love

Dancing Out Loud

9/30/21

To Margaret Virginia,

My dear friend may your Dancing Out Loud moments make you smile. When I think of 'Viz' I remember you and your kindness and it always makes me smile.

Love,
Elizabeth Moore

Also by Elaine Robnett Moore

The Art of Bead Stringing: Artist to Entrepreneur

Professional Jewellery Making With Beads

*Sixty Things I Have Found to Be True:
On the Occasion of My 60th Birthday*

Sweet Butterfly Wings

Dancing Out Loud

Thoughts on Navigating the Rhythms of Life

Elaine Robnett Moore

ERM Publications | Silver Spring, Maryland

ERM Publications, Silver Spring, MD

Copyright © 2020 by Elaine Robnett Moore
All rights reserved. No part of this book may be reproduced or transmitted in any form or by any means, electronic or mechanical, including photocopying, recording, or by any information storage and retrieval system, without permission in writing from the publisher.

ISBN: 9780990951834 (paperback)
ISBN: 9780990951827 (ebook)

CREDITS

Cover Design:
Vincent S. Barbre

Book Design and Formatting:
El-Lenor R. Barbre

Editing:
Chief Editor: El-Lenor R. Barbre
Contributing Editor: Peggy Bjamo
Developmental Editor: Judith Carlsson
Proofreading Editors: Bonnie Kramer & El-Lenor R. Barbre

Photography:
Jide Adeniyi-Jones
Susanne Ollmann
Zarmina Said
Bruce Weller
Elaine Robnett Moore

Captions:
Elaine Robnett Moore

Research:
Amber Melton
Elaine Robnett Moore

elainerobnettmoore.com

Dedication

This book is dedicated to my beautiful and talented grandchildren - Alisha & Leon, Chazmyn & Trey, Chelsey, Christian, Diane & Eric, Elisha LaDonna & Robert, Estefania, Etienne, Hugh Vincent, Kai & Maxxs, Krystle, Lance, Marcus, Mercedes & Dwight, Shaun & Brittany, Victor Jr., Zahra, and to my extended family Adetowo, Daniel, David, Korletey, Korlikie, Karen, Kevin, Mario, Victor, Gabriel, Alina, my great-grands - Adrian, Alexander, Amiya, Beaux, DeVonte, Dwight III, Inarae, Kaleb, Kalina Elaine, Landen, Leon, Nassiah, Selah, Shanmyn, Shaun Jr., Shayne, Trinity, to those who are to come, and to those who are a part of me in spirit.

You are the future of all that is and will be. You are artists, and scholars, and professionals, and soldiers, and dreamers, and scientists, and athletes, and educators. You are kind, strong, generous, compassionate, wise, curious, adventurous, happy, and surrounded by love.

I want you to know me, your Mimi, Nana, grandmother, grandma, auntie, great-grandmother, ancestor. I am the aggregate of our ancestors, as you will be to those who come after you. May the life force and wisdom of our ancestors that sustains me resonate prolifically in you. May it enable you to be outrageously strong, magnificently resilient, profusely confident in your art, abundantly assertive in your work, copiously competitive in your sport, brilliantly global in your thinking, opulent in your good-crazy, lavishly wiser, hugely passionate about life, excessively forgiving, profoundly peaceful, steadfastly devoted to family and always extravagantly loving.

I charge each of you to know and be at peace with who you are, where you come from, and who has been a part of your life. This knowledge will help you realize that you are exquisitely boundless in what you can achieve.

I celebrate you now and evermore.

Acknowledgments

My eternal gratitude to all those who played a role in the making of this book: to my grands and great-grands who were my inspiration, to Jabari and Liana Asim who encouraged me to do it and Jabari who gave me the structure for the chapters. To my very talented friends, Peggy Carr, Judy Carlsson, and Bonnie Kramer who reviewed and edited the book. To Ellie Barbre who managed, in the midst of giving birth to my latest cousin, moving from Los Angeles, CA to New Orleans, LA and in the end dodging a severe tropical storm, to do the final edit and all the formatting and design. To Vincent Barbre, Ellie's husband and a gifted artist, who designed the incredible cover of the book.

To Suzan Jenkins, Director of the Montgomery County Arts and Humanities Council, who carved time out of her busy schedule to write the Foreword. To my friends Linda Moore, Toni Dunton-Butler, Denise Benjamin, Malaika Pettigrew, Adhiambo Odaga, who enthusiastically helped to review chapters for me. To Bill Woodson, Torbjorn Carlsson and the women of the arts group, Assemblage, who were always there cheering me on. Collectively, they give truth to the phrase, "It takes a village."

Foreword

As an arts advocate and cultural warrior, I have spent a good majority of my life being astounded by the inimitable weight of the written word and the vast implications of a single drawing, a color, a performance, music, and works of art. It is both the precision of the intent, and the sweet, breezy afterglow of the picture painted, the image drawn, the notes, lingering ever so gently in the air, that inspires and connects me to the universe, friends, family and my community.

And although women have been shaping human history since the dawn of civilization, inspired in part by societal and political events aroused by economic and political discrimination, not many of us have a roadmap for life that documents the struggles, the pain, the strategies and the triumphs of those women, family members who paved the way for us.

And so it is with immense pleasure that I introduce you to Elaine Robnett Moore's work, seventy-five years in the making. This work - that of a master teacher, businesswoman, artist, mother, sister, daughter, auntie, grandmother, confidante, mentor and world traveler - is Elaine Robnett Moore's beautiful offering, that of a friend who has taken the time to put pen to paper about her life's dance.

Elaine Robnett Moore is a woman who has found joy and harnessed creativity in her literal and figurative journey. This book radiates and shares that joy, offering sweet lessons to savor as we consider the directions of the winds. Elaine's profound understanding of the world, enhanced by first-person experiences culled from working in communities across the globe, gives readers her worldwide insights that know no boundaries. And if there is anything I know for certain it is this, in order to achieve our life's truest potential, we must mightily work to liberate ourselves from fears and self-imposed barriers. In this way, we can free ourselves to explore the opportunities, avenues, lifestyles and possibilities, the dips and twirls that can lead us to a path that help us realize our true potential. By facing our fears and trusting our true selves, the possibilities are endless.

Thank you, Elaine, for this personal roadmap to help us see how to be free at the moment we wish to be and to encourage us to dance out loud...as though no one is watching.

-Suzan Jenkins

Suzan E. Jenkins is a leader in the non-profit arts and culture sector, a Peabody Award winning producer and an Executive Coach in Montgomery County, Maryland.

Introduction

This book reflects the wisdom of my ancestors, my grandparents - Hugh Glenn Robnett and Clara Pryer Robnett, Mildred Ponder Franklin and Irham (Boise) Franklin - the teachings of my parents - Elaine Franklin Robnett and Hugh Vincent Robnett - the enlightenment my children, Chanda, Vaughn & Claudia, Victor, Charmyn & Terry, Kai, grands, great-grands and extended family, Adhiambo, Awuor, Bessie, Diana and Diane have given me. The support of all my relatives, especially my aunt Lorraine, my sister Vinaida, my cousins Andrew, Genevieve & Hosea, Malaika & Andreâ, Sharon Romeo & Kevin, Linda Levy & David, and my friends, Linda Moore & Jackie Hughes, Rosemary Covington & Andre, Toni Dunton Butler, Cathy Royal, Gibwa Kajubi, Judy & Thor Carlsson, Maida Coleman, Janessa Herron, Hannelore & James McDaniel, Bill Woodson, Jabari & Liana Asim, William & Tracy Kelson, Denise Benjamin, Raesharn & Larry Beam, TeAntae Turner, Peggy Bjamo, Kathy Noble, Paul Hardy, Wendy Simmons, Lilia Abrom, Ellen Sweets, Eddie Laws, Sara Brown and more too numerous to name.

I am a woman who loves life! On the occasion of my sixtieth birthday, I wanted to surprise everyone by giving those I love a gift. I decided to put together sixty of the most important truths (in the form of quotes and observations) I had found to be helpful in the shaping of my life. I called it, *Sixty Things I Have*

Found to be True on the Occasion Of My Sixtieth Birthday. A truly profound title, don't you think?

I wrote it because I believe we should share what we find helpful to us as we attempt to navigate this world. When one writes about sixty anything it becomes a book by the sheer volume of the material itself. Since I have a large immediate and extended family, a book seemed the best way to reach everyone.

I especially wanted to share my insights with my children, grands, great grands, and beyond. To leave a record for my descendants that if they are curious they can know what I believed and dreamed. It may serve to explain why they have a tendency to be a little bit crazy or artistic, or stubborn. These are things I have always wondered about regarding my ancestors.

I am blessed to have some insight into my family history and know that I come from a long line of artists, among whom are *Alexandre Dumas, *pere* (father), a playwright and author who's books include *The Count of Monte Cristo*, *The Three Musketeers*, *The Black Tulip* and many more, his son, *Alexandre Dumas, *fils*, (son), also a successful novelist and playwright, *Francois M. Guyol de Guiran, who's paintings are at the Metropolitan Museum of Art in New York City, New York and the Art Museum in St. Louis, Missouri, *Tom Bass, saddlebred horse trainer in Mexico, Missouri who trained such famous horses as Belle Beach and Rex McDonald. *Mildred P. Franklin, (my grandmother on my mothers' side) who had the Mildred P. Franklin School of Dance in St. Louis, Missouri, and others who were quilters, bakers, poets, and musicians. We also had scientists, lawyers, and teachers like *Clara Robnett Scranage, a renowned astrophysicist. There are many pictures from as far back as the early 1800s, and some heirlooms. But there are no written words, that I am aware of, from the strong and brilliant women in my family.

The book, *Sixty Things,* was well received. So much so that I sought council from my good friend and author, *Jabari Asim, as to whether I should publish it in its original form. He suggested I take each quote and explain why or how I found it helpful, give an example and add pictures. I did. It just took me fifteen years to do it. In order to justify this delay, I have included insights reflective of the additional number of years it took to publish. I did add pictures and in true ERM form, the pictures are of pieces of my jewelry that I think reflect, in some way, the subject of the specific chapter it is in. This way you get a little bit of a few different parts of my artistic side. This is the result of what started sixteen years ago. I hope, at the least, you enjoy it and, at the most, you find it informative and entertaining.

I offer you this collection of thoughts, quotes, poems, pictures and experiences that have helped to shape, protect, guide, and comfort me. May they contribute to your well-being as well.

Alexandre Dumas - See Glossary
Alexandre Dumas, fils- See Glossary
Francois M. Guyol de Guiran - See Glossary
Tom Bass - See Glossary
Mildred P. Franklin - See Glossary
Clara Robnett Scranage - See Glossary
Jabari Asim - See Glossary

Table of Contents

DEDICATION VII
ACKNOWLEDGMENTS IX
FOREWORD X
INTRODUCTION XII
1   CELEBRATE NEW BEGINNINGS 1
2   SEEK WISDOM 5
3   SHARE YOUR WISDOM 11
4   ACKNOWLEDGE YOUR INNER DEITY 15
5   EMBRACE YOUR OWN PERFECTION 19
6   CLAIM YOUR DESTINY 23
7   NO COINCIDENCES... OPPORTUNITY IS KNOCKING 29
8   TRUST YOUR INTUITION 35
9   TRUST 41
10 BE HAPPY 47
11 CARE ENOUGH TO SMILE 51
12 LOVE IS HEART TO HEART 55
13 NINE DIMES DO NOT A DOLLAR MAKE 59
14 AMEN FOR THE CLEAN-UP-CREW 65
15 LOVE IS ETERNAL 69
16 YOU'LL NEVER LOVE THIS WAY AGAIN 75

17	ONCE UPON A TIME	79
18	ART IS THE BREATH OF LIFE	83
19	ART MIRACLES	87
20	DARE	93
21	WELCOME THE CHALLENGE	97
22	CARPE DIEM SEIZE THE DAY	103
23	NO LIMITATIONS	109
24	RECOGNIZE THE GOOD	113
25	LET GO, LET GOD, LET THE UNIVERSE	117
26	HIS EYE IS ON THE SPARROW	121
27	JOY IS SHARING	125
28	QUIET DETERMINATION PREVAILS	129
29	SHARE YOUR WEALTH	133
30	BE GRATEFUL	137
31	MINDFULNESS	141
32	NEVER BURN BRIDGES	147
33	DARE TO DREAM	151
34	STAY ALERT	155
35	EXPECT A MIRACLE	159
36	ACCEPT RESPONSIBILITY	163
37	GIVE WHAT YOU WOULD KEEP	167
38	CONSIDER YOURSELF HUGGED	171
39	HONOR YOURSELF, RELEASE PAIN	175

40	LIFE ROCKS	179
41	WORDS ARE PROFOUND GIFTS	183
42	EXPRESS YOURSELF THROUGH POETRY	189
43	THINK, THEN SPEAK OR WRITE	195
44	GO HIGH	199
45	TRUTH TRIUMPHS	205
46	CHERISH YOUR FAMILY AND FRIENDS	209
47	BE SPONTANEOUS	213
48	INNER BEAUTY IS EVERLASTING	219
49	STAND TALL	223
50	GET OUT OF YOUR OWN WAY	227
51	BE OPEN, BE OBSERVANT, LISTEN	231
52	IT'S OK TO CHANGE YOUR MIND	235
53	SOLITUDE	241
54	YOU REAP WHAT YOU SOW	245
55	PROTECT THE CHILDREN	251
56	GUARDIANS	255
57	HONOR YOUR GUARDIANS	261
58	SISTERHOOD	267
59	MY SISTAS	273
60	BROTHERHOOD	277
61	LIVE EVERY ADVENTURE	281
62	CELEBRATE DIFFERENCES	285

63	GRASP LIFE	291
64	DANCE	295
65	BE CRAZY	299
66	FORGIVE	305
67	LOSS	309
68	BE PRESENT	315
69	BE FOCUSED	319
70	PRAY FOR THE LION	323
71	PASSION	329
72	EMBRACE YOUR INDIOSYNCRASIES	333
73	10 DEGREES OF EASY	339
74	BE ENLIGHTENED	343
75	CARRY ON	349
76	THE ELEPHANT IN THE ROOM	353
77	GETTING A HOLD ON OUR HUMANITY	361
78	GUARDIANSHIP OF EARTH	367
79	KINDNESS	373
80	I AM A BUTTERFLY	379
81	LEGACY	385

ABOUT THE AUTHOR 388

GLOSSARY 390

Necklace - Smooth Jazz - Rubber, Shell, Faux Sinew

1

Celebrate New Beginnings

Elaine Robnett Moore

> *"What the caterpillar calls the end of the world,
> the Master calls a butterfly...."*
> *-Richard Bach*

This quote is a major linchpin in the foundation of my life. Once upon a time, someone very special gave me a copy of the book, *Illusions,* by Richard Bach. This quote is found in the book as well as several other quotes that I find helpful. In times when things look the bleakest, or when the world seems to be crashing around you, think about this. It is at these moments that we should look for the bigger picture. Every ending is a new beginning. A beginning that is something greater, more beautiful, and more fulfilling than anything you can imagine.

In my life, there are thousands of examples, some big, some small, which validate these words. The following one resonates because it reminds me of how different my life would be, but for the turn of events that brought me to this place.

I owned a travel agency. I bought it, convinced it was what I wanted to do for the rest of my life. I loved arranging travel for individuals and groups. I loved working as a tour operator, and convention and meeting planner, as well as traveling with groups and assuring that my clients' travels were without incident. However, after a few years, with the introduction of the Internet and discount travel packages, the business began losing momentum. In addition, as much as I loved working with people, I detested the endless bookkeeping part of the business. Had it not eventually become necessary to close it, I don't think I would be here now, creating amazing jewelry, teaching, writing, and consulting. In a million years, I could not have dreamed of anything as enjoyable, rewarding, and fulfilling as being the artist I have become.

To be clear though, at that time, that moment in time, I thought all was lost. I thought it was the end of the world. What saved me was this quote. It kept me open. It allowed me to see new possibilities, new beginnings.

Look for the butterfly.

Elaine Robnett Moore

* Necklace - Ancient Wisdom - Baltic Amber, Fossilized Coral, Sterling Silver, Rubber

2

Seek Wisdom

Elaine Robnett Moore

> *"The universe is yours if you choose to have it.*
> *Of course, you have to know what to do with it."*
> -erm

The wisdom you need to successfully claim the gifts this universe has for you, comes from amazing sources. I have learned from my elders, my children, my grandchildren, friends, strangers, nature, books, and the Internet. When I have been open, the solutions came easily. When I have resisted because I was not willing to allow that someone younger, or older, or smarter, or not so smart could possibly know more than me, those are the times I have failed to learn what I needed to know. Those are the lessons I have had to repeat until I was ready to listen and learn. Save yourself steps and some grief, stay open and accept each gift of wisdom when it is offered to you.

When I was young I listened to my elders. Now I listen to my grands. They have so many lessons. There is so much to learn.

I have found that an easy way to acknowledge the solution to an issue when it is presented to me is to laugh at how obvious it should have been for me to figure it out. I get the biggest kick out of realizing that, on occasion, here I am the teacher being taught by my student. This way I can enjoy the way the universe chooses to reveal the wisdom I seek. I am reminded to be humble, to stay open, and most of all, to enjoy that no matter where the wisdom I seek comes from, I am open to receiving it.

One such lesson came from my son, Victor, when he was about six years of age. I had promised to take my children to a drive-in movie one summer evening. For those of you who are not familiar with what this is, let me explain. It is an outdoor theatre where you stay in your car. At that time, you drove up to a post, took a speaker off the post, then attached it to your car and watched the movie. This was a great thing because you could take the children in their nightclothes and carry your own snacks. But I digress.

I had checked the weather and it was threatening to rain. I explained to my children that we should postpone the outing until another night. Victor said to wait a minute and went out onto the front porch of our home and looking up at the heavens said, "God, please don't let it rain. We want to go to the movies." The clouds parted. My son said, "It's OK we can go now; it won't rain." Since it did look as if it would not rain for a while, I reluctantly said ok.

When we got to the drive-in and got situated, just as the movie started, a few drops of rain hit the windshield. I said to Victor, "I think we are going to have to go because it's going to rain after all." He said, "Wait a minute, mom." He rolled the window on the car down, sat on the window ledge, leaned out, hands in the prayer position, looked up, and said, "Not yet, Lord, the movie isn't over."

The rain stopped. We watched the movie, and the rain didn't start up again until we were getting out of the car at home. That night my son taught me the power of prayer when you have absolute faith. There is profound truth in the Zen proverb, "When the student is ready, the teacher will come."

Seek wisdom.

Elaine Robnett Moore

* Necklace - Jungle Fever - Handblown Glass, Kola Nuts, Wood, Sterling Silver, Faux Sinew

3

Share Your Wisdom

"Some things you know and take for granted are often the very bits of wisdom a person you encounter has been waiting for or needs to know."
-erm

Share what you know to be true with those who are in your life, those who come into your life, and those who cross your path. We all carry messages, insights, or bits of wisdom for others. We don't have to know them or understand the message or the wisdom. We simply have to stay open and willing to share what we know, or sometimes, what comes to us. The key is to be open to both receive and to share. Be careful though, to pass on the thoughts that come to you, as they come to you. Do not attempt to influence others with what you want them to do, only share the information as it comes to you. This may sound a bit tricky, but practice makes perfect and it is doable.

While talking to someone, have you ever shared a random thought only to have that person say, "Wow! How did you know that was exactly the thing I was concerned about", or, "What you just said is the answer to what has been bothering me"?

Share your skills. After all, they hold bits of wisdom as well. Do not hold back because you are afraid that if you share all you know, the other person will take it to a level you have not reached. Share because you want them to go as far as possible. Remember that there really is nothing new in the world. Whatever you are sharing is part of a continuum. It happened before and it will happen again. I believe that the failure to share your gifts can cause you to lose them. Alternatively, the more you give, the more you gain.

There was a moment when I first started making jewelry that I often think of. I met a young woman, Adhiambo, through a mutual friend of ours. We were living in the same building. She is my daughters' age, collected exquisite African art and loved unusual jewelry, especially those pieces made from African trade beads. When I first made jewelry all of my pieces had African trade beads in them, as these beads were the reason I was obsessed with making jewelry.

One day, she came by to see what I was working on and she noticed I was struggling with a man-made material called imitation sinew (in my pieces, I refer to it as faux sinew). While I had discovered this fiber was perfect for stringing trade beads, I had yet to master the best ways to incorporate it in my designs. She looked at what I was doing and said, "Why don't you twist it?" I said, "I didn't think it would hold up over time." She said, "Sure it will. I'll show you." She did and faux sinew became the main staple to my core designs for several years. Now, I teach how to work with it worldwide.

Over the years our friendship morphed into a bond as close as family. There are days when she learns much from me, and days when I learn much from her. It began with the twist of that thread.

Share your wisdom.

Elaine Robnett Moore

* Necklace - Glam - Bi Lemon / Smoky Quartz, Onyx, Rubber, Swarovski Pearls

4

Acknowledge Your Inner Deity

*"Don't be afraid to see yourself as a goddess or god.
Your Creator already does."*
-erm

How many times have you heard or read that a deity lives inside each of us? For me this is true. To be one with your God is to accept that there is a Force that lives in each of us, and that we are one with 'It', as 'It' is a part of us. In acknowledgement of this oneness, we must, at all times, be respectful of and honor who we are. This should put a literal meaning to the expression, "your body is your temple."

Pay attention to what you are passionate about, and the things in life you love. Explore them; determine what possibilities they hold that you can turn into a business, a career, a vocation, a job, or a hobby. Recognize how your passions can help you find your core strengths.

From time to time there will be moments when you stray from what you know, in the core of your being, to be correct for you in thought, word, or deed. You doubt your self-worth or your ability to discern what is right for you.

There may be times when you think the only path to success is to follow someone else's dream, whether the dream is their dream for themselves or one they have for you. These are obstacles you must overcome; use them as stepping-stones. These stepping-stones are in your life to help you grow. Embrace them. Let them be a part of your own solid foundation. Neither God nor this Universe makes mistakes. Everyone and everything has a purpose. Remember that what works for someone else is not necessarily what will work for you or vice versa. Find your truth, and your reason for being.

For the longest time I thought I was supposed to be a mother and a businesswoman. I love being a mother. I enjoy being a businesswoman. It didn't, in the beginning, register with me, that in the middle of children and business there was always art. Invariably, I could be found jotting down words for a poem, decorating an office, or helping my children with art projects. The poetry would come to me at the oddest times - on a plane headed to a meeting, in the waiting room of a doctor's office, or looking out over the ocean. It was years before I paid attention. It took beads entering my life to wake me up. It took the Universe giving me a shove for me to realize that my joy, my peace, is in my family and my art. Now, I put a little business sense into my family and my art and my world is complete.

For those who do not believe in God, give this energy or this force any name you wish. It is the power at the core of your being. It is what drives and directs you. Recognize it, embrace it, and use it. It enables us to be our highest selves.

Acknowledge your inner deity.

Elaine Robnett Moore

* Necklace - Sweet Blues - A. Styles Polymer Clay, Swarovski Crystal, Rubber, Bronze

5

Embrace Your Own Perfection

Elaine Robnett Moore

"I believe everyone / everything in the Universe is perfect."
-erm

Who are we to decide what perfection is? How can we possibly identify it? I suggest you look in the mirror and if you are visually challenged, feel the contours of your face. Each of us has our own perfection - out of the shower, no designer clothes, no make-up, no haircut, yet, simply perfection.

No one can define perfection for someone else. There are as many different versions as there are people on this planet. What you see as a handicap in someone else, that person sees as a blessing. What you see as a disadvantage in me, I see as an advantage.

There are no two of us that are exactly alike so there is no one idea of perfect. We are of different cultures, ethnicities, states of health, size, knowledge, religious beliefs, etc. Not one of these things alters our individual perfection. When we define the best as having one definition, we limit our own ability to be fearless and boundless. We create a negative field around us that restricts what we can accomplish.

I have migraine headaches and carpal tunnel syndrome. When I first started making jewelry I registered with Very Special Arts (VSA), an organization that works with artists with disabilities. A few years ago, I was asked by the Department of Labor if I would be willing to be featured as a disabled artist in a pamphlet they were putting together. I called the ex-director of VSA and told her I had concerns because neither my migraines nor carpal tunnel syndrome had ever stopped me from doing anything I wanted, including making jewelry. I said to her there were others who were clearly more limited than me, based on their disabilities. I will always remember what she said. "Well, you don't have to acknowledge that you are disabled if you don't want to. But you are, by definition, disabled. The fact that you do not allow it to interfere with your life is exactly why they want you to be a part of this promotion." I did agree to be featured in the Department of Labor's Pamphlet.

Embrace who you are, as you are, at this moment in time, as the perfect being you are. Do not allow someone else's label to define your perfection. Bear in mind that this perfection that is you may change from time to time. You may lose or gain weight. You may lose a limb. You may gain knowledge or a sense of humor. You may suffer mental challenges. It doesn't matter. You are whole, beautiful, and perfect just the way you are at this moment and every moment in time. You have no boundaries.

Embrace your own individual perfection.

Elaine Robnett Moore

* *Necklace - Puff the Magic Dragon - Polymer Clay, Silver & Brass, Swarovski Crystal, Rubber*

6

Claim Your Destiny

> *"Know your Inner Spirit.*
> *Recognize the power that dwells within you.*
> *Follow the intuitive guidance of your Inner Being."*
> *-erm*

Wake up! Pay attention! You already have the answers you need in life. Just be still long enough to hear them, feel them, and recognize them. It's amazing what we can learn when we are still and open.

We often seek answers from everywhere but within. We believe that we could not possibly be smart enough or intuitive enough to know the answers. After all, who are we? You may believe only the learned and wise have the answers to life's questions. Wrong. I believe we are born with most of the answers we will need in our lifetimes. Some we gain along life's highway. We have to learn how to recognize them. They are safely tucked away until we are ready to know their truth, and acknowledge our power.

Often, doing a little homework to unlock our personal treasure chest can access the solution we hold inside. The process of inquiry is the first step.

- What questions arise in you?
- What are the solutions you are exploring?
- Are problems being tackled?
- What answers are being found?

Most importantly, be open to recognizing the truth when it manifests itself. Be still and listen.

One example of when education did not equate to wisdom was when I was asked to serve on the board of a southern university. I had hesitated to say yes as I felt ill-equipped to serve with such accomplished academics. After a bit of persuasion from the university president, I agreed. At one of my first board meetings, a primary agenda item to be addressed was the roofs repairs on four of the campus buildings. One of the professors had taken on the task of getting bids from the local contractors to assess the work needed and to submit proposals for the repairs. He very proudly gave his report, which read as follows: "I sent requests for bids to do the repairs of four of our buildings to seven local contractors and had the newspaper run an ad for a 'request for proposals.' I am happy to report that we received several bids. Of the bids, there were three whose credentials and references met our standards."

I am not giving you the actual numbers involved in the bids, as I do not remember them. I am giving you hypothetical figures as an example, which does reflect the problem I had with the conclusion of the professor's report.

The professor went on to sum up his report by saying, "The three bids to repair the four roofs were respectively, $300,000.00, $150,000.00 and $50,000.00. You will be pleased to know I am recommending we accept the lowest bid of $50,000."

I waited for someone to raise questions and no one did. So I did. I was reluctant to say anything as these were all scholars and I wasn't, but I had to. I asked if all the contractors had been given the same specifications, had all of them worked on projects of this size before and finally, were they all bonded? I went on to explain that the bids were so far apart that it warranted closer scrutiny. I further stated that the lowest bid was the least equipped to execute the contract. I explained how the discrepancy in the range of the bids of the three contractors could mean that they were either all working together or maybe two of them had no clue what they were doing. We ended up going with the highest bid. It was the only one that could back up what they had proposed with figures that supported their bid.

When you know you are correct or believe you are, you have to stand up, state what you know to be true, and back it up with your reasoning. I assure you, I hesitated to say anything because I found it hard to believe that these learned individuals didn't see the flaws in the initial report, that they didn't see the disparity among the three bids was simply too large to be ignored.

When you feel you are right or have useful information or ideas to contribute, then do so. It is your duty to question and to present alternative options.

There is an easy way to confirm you are on the right track. Once you have listened to your inner voice, listen to what those around you say. In a group situation, my test is that if three people independently mirror what I was thinking, I take it as confirmation that I should at least explore the possibilities.

When you think you have an answer, say it. If you have a contribution, make it. And if you have a question, ask it. The most important answers emerge when one is courageous enough to ask questions.

Claim your destiny.

Elaine Robnett Moore

* *Necklace - Shangri-La - Brass, Baltic Amber, Wood, Swarovski Crystal Pearls, Rubber*

7

No Coincidences... Opportunity Is Knocking

Elaine Robnett Moore

> *"There are no coincidences.
> There is a reason for everyone who crosses your path.
> Stay alert so you recognize opportunity when it
> knocks, whispers, shouts, calls, or texts."*
> *-erm*

There is an expression that speaks to missed opportunities. It is, "Sometimes you can't see the forest for the trees." Translated this means, we are presented with opportunities all the time and quite often we don't recognize them.

In my world, every time I meet anyone, no matter their position or station in life, it presents an occasion to explore new possibilities. How often have you looked back and realized that a chance encounter resulted in a lifelong friendship, or the resolution to a situation you had labored over. When least you expect it, opportunity knocks.

My best example happened four months after I started making jewelry. A friend arranged an introduction for me to meet the owner of an African clothing store in Washington, D.C. I contacted the owner and set up an appointment to come to his store and show him my jewelry. The idea was that if he liked my work he would agree to purchase pieces to be sold in his store.

Dancing Out Loud

On the appointed day, I arrived on time for our meeting and was excited about the possible outcome, only to find out he and his wife had gone to New York City to buy merchandise for the store. He had forgotten about the appointment. The gentleman who was taking care of the store identified himself as the owner's best friend. (It is in these moments when it is hard to remember that something good comes out of everything.) So, I asked him if he would be kind enough to look at my work and let the owner know what he thought about it. That way if he didn't like it he could convey that to the owner. This would enable the owner to bow out of meeting with me and save both of us some time.

He agreed. While he waited on other customers I laid out the pieces I had brought. He looked at them, liked them, and asked if I had thought about showing them to the Smithsonian Museums. I thanked him and said that I didn't know anyone at the Smithsonian. I explained that I was not comfortable cold calling (a sales term that means calling on someone without an introduction) the buyers for the Smithsonian stores.

He said, "Well if you knew someone in the National Museum of African Art Gift Shop would you consider that a good enough connection?" I assured him I would. He said, "Well, I am the manager of the National Museum of African Art Gift Shop." He then proceeded to give me the buyer's name and number and suggested I use his name when I called. I did, and as a result, my pieces were sold at the Smithsonian's National Museum of African Art, the Renwick Gallery, the Arts and Industry Museum and the National Museum of Natural History for several years.

The lesson - open the door when opportunity is knocking. Be creative. If the front door is locked, try the back door or the window. Sometimes, an unexpected path will lead to a better outcome. Be flexible, don't give up, and leave the door open. After all, the Universe awaits the joy you can bring.

Opportunity is knocking.

Elaine Robnett Moore

* Necklace - Journey - A. Styles Polymer Clay, Faux Sinew, Sterling Silver

8

Trust Your Intuition

Elaine Robnett Moore

"Pay attention to your Inner Voice, Spirit, Divine Self. Remember, your first thought is usually the right one."
-erm

Should you have doubts, let's run a little test. Think of the times you have had a premonition concerning something you were about to embark upon. When you paid attention to those feelings or listened to your inner voice, all went well. When you did not, things often turned out to be a hot mess. I learned a long time ago, to listen to my inner voice. I have many examples of how this works. The following is just one.

Several years ago, I had to drive one of my then teenage daughters to the airport in St. Louis, Missouri. This was before the airport security we know of today, so one could arrive, literally, minutes before the flight and go straight to the gate. As usual for me in those days, I had left my office late to pick up my daughter to get her to the airport. There were two routes I could take. The one I usually took was west on Highway 40 (it was scenic and I thought safer). The other was west on Highway 70, which went through a rougher part of the city and had a history of more accidents. There was a point at which I had to decide which route I would take. When I reached the cross road, my intuition said turn right and take Highway 70. Because I had already learned to listen, I turned right. My daughter asked, "Why are you going this way?" I replied, "something tells me it is the best way to go today." Since all my children were familiar with my beliefs (they were very tolerant children), she said OK.

Within ten minutes of the airport, in the middle lane of the highway and going about sixty miles per hour, one of my tires blew out. This left my Chrysler station wagon with no power steering. The car started to swerve dangerously. My daughter nervously asked, "Are we going to be OK?" to which I responded, "yes, your seat belt is fastened, and we took the route we were supposed to take." I regained control of the car. Immediately, there was an exit and the other lanes were empty, and with difficulty, I was able to move over three lanes and take the exit.

This exit was in a residential area where it would be unusual for commercial businesses to be located. By the way, this was before cell phones, which limited my ability to get help. My daughter asked, "Am I still going to make my flight?" "Absolutely," I said, and once again, I stated that by taking the route intuitively designated meant everything would work out. My daughter relaxed, waiting to see how she was going to make the flight.

As we got to the end of the exit ramp, there in the middle of this quiet residential area was an auto repair shop. We were about six minutes away from the airport, with ten minutes to get to the gate. There sat a taxi parked on the lot of the auto repair shop. I pulled into the garage lot, went in and asked for the driver of the taxi. I should mention that I had forgotten to take my wallet when I left the office. All I had was a ten-dollar bill.

The taxi driver said ten dollars would get my daughter to the airport. I kissed her goodbye, put her in the taxi, and off she went.

Now there was the issue of my car. I went back into the garage and asked the attendant if I could please use his phone. I needed to call my office to have someone bring my wallet to pay for the repair of the tire. He said, "You don't remember me, but two years ago I attended a lecture on entrepreneurship you gave at the Forest Park Community College in St. Louis." He told me that it was because of that lecture that he had decided to open the auto repair shop, saying he had always wanted to thank me, so fixing my tire was the least he could do.

The blown tire did not cause an accident, my daughter made her flight, the tire was repaired and I met someone whose life had been changed because of something I had said years before. All because I listened to that inner voice!

Trust your intuition.

Elaine Robnett Moore

* Necklace - Steps - Amber, Tiger Eye, Copper, Bone, Rubber

Dancing Out Loud

9

Trust

"Love all, trust a few, do wrong to none."
-Shakespeare

The fundamental ingredient in a healthy relationship, whether personal or professional, is trust. It is the bedrock on which a solid foundation can be built.

Trust starts when you love yourself. This is the first truth, for each of us. If you do not love yourself, then your journey begins with you doing the homework necessary to gain self-knowledge. Look inside yourself, seek the reasons you do not feel good about who you are and determine what you need to do to fall in love with you. Once you begin to see the why of you, you will begin to see that behind the curtain is the beautiful person you are.

Think about what makes you smile. Are you kind? Are you generous? Are you patient? Embrace these qualities and accept each one that applies as proof of why you are worthy of your own love and of being loved. Do not set the bar so high that only a saint could reach it. Realize that what you can't fix, you can manage. Recognize that all of us at one point or another doubt our value. Understanding who you are is becoming self-aware. You are becoming the self you will be happy to live with the rest of your life. The beauty of self-love is that it attracts the kind of love you desire from others.

> *"Trust starts with truth and ends with truth."*
> *-Santosh Kalwar*

The confidence that is evident in one who has reached self-awareness encourages the trust of others in you. Most importantly, it improves your ability to recognize those who are reputable. You can trust that you will usually do what is right by others.

You are only as good as your word. Keep your word. When you keep your word, whether by being truthful, on time for appointments, honoring contracts you enter into, or promises you make, you build trust and loyalty.

Does the fact that you are trustworthy mean that no one will ever be dishonest with you? No. But one individual is not the whole human race and should not stop you from believing in others. Rely on your intuition to tell you whom to trust. On the occasion of trusting the wrong person, review the situation and see if you can figure out the lesson it contains. It will help to keep you from repeating the same mistake.

I had a business partner who professed often to be a righteous, church-going woman. This person hired someone she knew to be dishonest, and a large sum of money was stolen from our office. I had trusted her. Had I listened to my intuition, I would never have given her any power. It was a mistake.

What is relevant to this story is that an investigation was initiated. The investigator, a retired FBI agent, indicated he was confident he could find collusion in the theft between my business partner, our employee and me. As I responded to him, he questioned my professional background. In the process of his inquiry, he realized he knew who I was. I was able to confirm I had built a housing complex and he knew my solid ethical and professional background.

He then confirmed that he had been with the FBI during the time I was co-developer of the housing complex. He went on to say, the agency had investigated my company and me. They had gone so far as to put someone in my office to determine what exactly was going on. During the course of these questions his tone changed from suspicion to one of cautious respect. He said that they had been amazed at how my company had operated without a hint of scandal in what they considered to be a questionable environment. He then said, "I will get into this case and let you know in a few days what I have found."

When he called back a few days later, it was to tell me that his office had cleared me of any involvement. Had my previous work not validated that I was trustworthy, the outcome might not have been as good. The agent might not have done as thorough an investigation as he did, and the result could have been different. While it was a costly lesson, it was a lesson on listening to my intuitive self, the importance of being trustworthy, and always vetting potential employees.

Trust starts with truth.

Elaine Robnett Moore

* Necklace - Jacobs Ladder - Wood, Seeds, Swarovski Crystal, Sterling Silver, Rubber

10

Be Happy

Elaine Robnett Moore

"No one is responsible for your happiness but you."
-Randy

I must have been around forty before I began to truly understand that happiness comes from within, not without. Therefore, the only one who can make you happy is you! A big step in the right direction is finding joy and happiness in little things.

One of the biggest obstacles to finding happiness is expecting it to be delivered to us when we already are surrounded by it. My joy, and yours, comes from within. It's waking up in the morning and seeing a ray of sunlight or hearing a bird sing. It doesn't matter whether you literally see it, or sense the changes in nature that surround you. It matters that you laugh at yourself, and that you can feel life. Some days, it's not the big things that we think we need like fireworks or circuses, or a significant other. It is the sweet, personal, gentle touches of happiness that fill our days and nights with music. It is the touch of color, and love, and dance, and song, and hugs, and smiles, and tears, and puppies, and guinea pigs. It is stars in the sky, and memories, and, always, laughter. These things make us smile in spite of our determination to define happiness in grandiose ways that are not nearly as fulfilling or lasting, and sometimes, not readily obtainable. It is the little things that invariably lead us to our individual joy! It is these memories that will and do sustain us throughout our lives.

I learned one of my best lessons about happiness from a dear friend, many years ago. I would say to him from time to time that he made me happy. He would always say to me, "I am not responsible for your happiness. Each of us is responsible for our own happiness." Back then I didn't understand it. Now I know he spoke the truth.

Choose to be happy.

Elaine Robnett Moore

* *Necklace - Carnival - Hand Blown, Glass, Swarovski Crystal, Rubber, Sterling Silver*

11

Care Enough to Smile

Elaine Robnett Moore

> *"Give a smile to all you encounter along life's pathways. Sometimes your smile may be the only good thing that happens to an individual that day, week, month..."*
> *-erm*

A smile is one of the best gifts we can give and it costs us only the desire and willingness to share a single beautiful moment with a friend or a total stranger. It can be a simple expression of greeting, a hello, or it can convey joy, peace, hope, love, wisdom, and sometimes, pain.

Pay attention to what happens to you when you smile at someone. Notice your step becomes a little lighter. Negative things around you fade into the background. Sometimes, the very person you smiled at smiles back! Isn't it amazing how contagious smiles are? It's shocking how one smile can generate so much pure positive energy! You know what? There are moments when there is no one around, and I smile just for me! Oh - another interesting fact - people remember a sincere smile long after you leave the room.

When I was about nine years old, I walked into a room at home pouting. My adult cousin, *David, who was visiting, looked at me and said, "You should always smile no matter how upset or angry you are. When you smile it makes you beautiful and you light up the space around you. When you frown you look ugly and those who see you are guarded and not interested in hearing why you are frowning." He was right. He was someone I respected and admired. His words registered. I will always be grateful to him for sharing wisdom that has served me well throughout my life.

Care enough to smile.

* *David James - See Glossary*

*Necklace - Fire Dreams - Baltic Amber, Vintage Glass, Garnets, Swarovski Crystal, Faux Sinew

12

Love Is Heart to Heart

Elaine Robnett Moore

"Heart to heart is unconditional."
-erm

It is your family and your friends who will always be there for you. They will carry you through the darkness and lift you into the light. They will dance with you in purple rain, or sail with you across uncharted seas. They will shout the truth to you until you hear it or be still with you until you see it. They will bring you rainbows to wrap your sorrow in, or butterflies to release your joy. These things they do for you. These things you do for them. And best of all, they will love you and you will love them back.

It is difficult to accept unconditional love when we think we are unworthy. Remember, the key word here is 'unconditional' so we don't get to put conditions on this love or restrict it. We do get to be grateful it is being given to us. We do get to embrace and celebrate it.

Many times, I have met people and known instantly that there was a connection, a love, that didn't make sense in the textbook way. Yet, spiritually it existed and was real. One such friend was a woman I met on the platform of the Metro (subway system) in Silver Spring, Maryland. Both of us were waiting for the train, standing not too far from each other. I noticed her because she was wearing a beautiful scarf. I pondered over whether or not to tell her what a lovely scarf she was wearing. Finally, I did tell her. She smiled and said, "Thank you, I have been admiring your earrings." I told her that I designed jewelry and taught jewelry making. She was from Lebanon and wanted to learn how to make jewelry. The train came and we boarded. We sat together and though her English was limited and my Arabic non-existent, we talked and exchanged contact information.

We became friends. We lived close to each other and visited back and forth. She would invite me to wonderful Lebanese dinners with her and her husband. Always at the end, she would produce a tray with carnelian and hematite beads and ask me how she should go about designing a necklace for this friend or that relative.

It became a pleasant challenge for me to determine how many different ways one can string the same size carnelian and hematite beads. She never took a class from me, but I loved the game we played and the friendship we had. It was a beautiful friendship until one day she was gone. Still I think of her from time to time and I always smile.

Love is heart to heart.

Elaine Robnett Moore

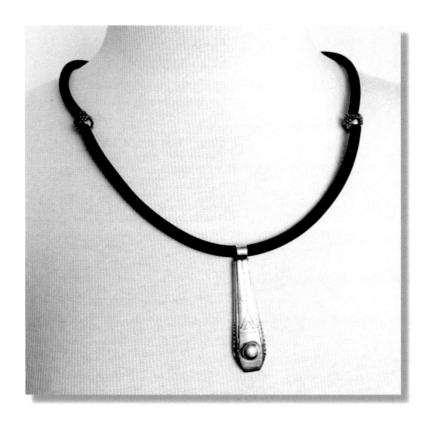

* *Necklace - Lightening - Sterling Silver, Rubber*

13

Nine Dimes Do Not a Dollar Make

> *"Never settle for less, in a partner,
> than the truth that is you."*
> *-erm*

You may compromise on some issues. This is good. You may need to allow time for your partner and you to grow into a perfect pair. Coming together on many issues, while respecting the unique individuality of each of you. But at no time will one who loves you ever ask you to compromise or lower your values or morals. Nor should you.

> *"You don't need someone to complete you,
> you only need someone to accept you completely."*
> *-Anonymous*

The one question I am often asked is, "How will you know who is or isn't the right person for you?" The answer is, you just know. You may not want to admit it, but you absolutely already know. In the core of your being, in your soul, in your brain, you know.

When it is not the right person, there is that uneasiness that just won't go away. There is that something just out of touch, that you can't quite put words to that raises doubt. There is a problem if you have to keep making excuses for them. Excuses like why they are not with you at important events. Why they are uneasy around your family. Why you haven't met their family or friends yet after a period of dating. Why you cannot reach them easily by phone. These questions help you accept the answer you already know. NO! This is not the right person for you. But, you already knew.

If you are not uneasy, nothing is out of touch, and you don't have serious doubts, then keep going. Maybe this is the right one. At the least it is worth exploring further.

I went to my friend Joe (a seer) once and said to him, "Joe I met this really great guy. He is tall, caring, worldly, etc. However there are a few little things I am not comfortable with." He said, "He sounds like a nice person but always remember, nine dimes do not a dollar make." I have never forgotten these wise words. At the end of the day, if a dollar is what you need, nine dimes won't do. Keep looking.

In honor of this truth, I wrote a poem called, "You are Not the One." Here is the last verse:

Elaine Robnett Moore

It's a crime and a shame
You being
So close to perfect
But no matter
How you rearrange the change
Nine dimes do not a dollar make

AND YOU ARE NOT THE ONE

Nine dimes do not a dollar make.

Elaine Robnett Moore

* *Necklace - Supreme - Brass, Agate, Wood, Faux Sinew*

14

Amen for the Clean-up-Crew

Elaine Robnett Moore

> *"Lovers may come and go.
> Friends remain to help you pick up the piece."*
> -erm

The good news is you have a clean-up-crew. They are the ones who are there when you are disappointed, devastated and feeling bad. Par for the course, anyone who dares to step out into the world of dating is likely to have experienced this.

Some person will come into your life who has a nice outer wrapper but no depth. Deep down this person, for many reasons, may not even be capable of loving a partner and needs therapy. Narcissism is but one personality disorder that will cause a person to hurt you. This is the poor excuse of a human being that leaves us in need of a clean-up-crew. This description may sound a little harsh, but not to those who have experienced someone who fits some aspect of the above profile.

This crew is composed of your best friends, best buds, text pals, phone friends, sometimes your mentor, your mother, your grandmother or work friends (though, I suggest you keep your personal business out of the workplace). Once you let them know what is or has happened they come - via text, email, phone, or in person - and right away you begin to feel better.

The ever-present danger is that you don't let them know. You allow your pride or embarrassment to get in the way of your common sense. Reach out and touch base with those who care about you. They have the power to lift you up and help you put things back into perspective. Do you know why they have this ability? Because everyone has been where you are at one time or another!

Be aware that if someone you reach out to only wants to tell you that they knew it all the time, but did not say anything, or suggest that you must have been blindfolded not to see. Quietly move away from them. They do not have your best interest at heart.

There was the time I dated a man that I discovered was seeing other women while we were supposed to be an exclusive couple. When I brought his infidelity to his attention, he explained to me that he was doing me a favor. By going out with these women, he was showing them that I was the better woman because he would always come back to me.

Now my friends, believe it or not, because I really liked him and had wanted him to be the one, I had to work hard to say, "You have to go. I deserve so much better than you." Would you believe he could not understand why I had ended our relationship? Still, it really hurt to walk away.

My friends were there. It was a difficult time. They took turns holding my hand, listening to me cry and reminding me to laugh. Most importantly, they were there to help me. One friend, RoseMary, reminded me that I was worth so much more than this totally challenged boy in a man's body. I stayed strong and didn't take him back.

Amen for the clean-up-crew.

Elaine Robnett Moore

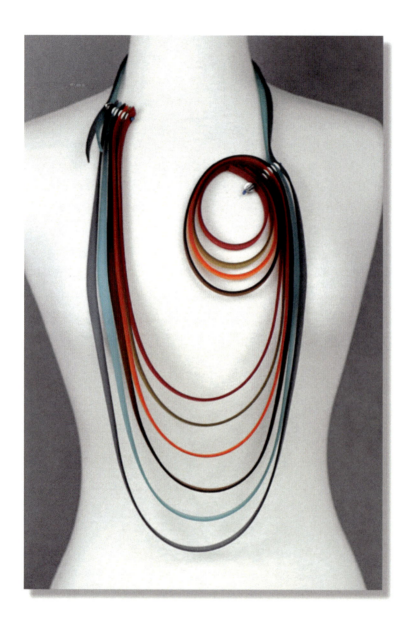

* Necklace - Symphony - Rubber, Faux Sinew

15

Love Is Eternal

Elaine Robnett Moore

> *"Love is everlasting. It is impossible to lose a loved one.*
> *They never leave us. We carry them with us*
> *in our hearts, in our spirits, always."*
> *-erm*

You are the continued manifestation of the good of those you love who are here, and those who have transitioned. You hear their words of wisdom when you need to. You know they are there when you hear their favorite song or quote at just the right moment. You see an object they cherished, or that had special meaning for the two of you. Suddenly, there is the scent of their cologne, their clothing or their pipe tobacco. Your ancestors and your loved ones never leave you.

Love transcends time and space. It permeates one's whole being. It takes you to heights some only dream of. When you are in love, you want everyone to experience this high, this euphoric state of being at one with the Universe. It is so powerful, so profound, so fulfilling, that once you've experience it, you can be at peace if you never get there again. My favorite saying is, "If you have been to the mountain once and never get there again, it's OK. Once is more than enough."

The love of a soulmate is enough to last a thousand lifetimes. The spirit of this love will speak to your heart before your mind can comprehend this wonder. Yes. It is a little scary to open up and be vulnerable, but what would life be without risk?

There are seven kinds of love, each kind with its own gifts for you. Some people will experience all of the types listed, while others will only know some of them. Each of us is on this earth to learn lessons specific to whom we are and what we want to know. We seek answers. So, you experience the love necessary for you to grow, to dream, and to be whole. Welcome it and recognize it is exactly the kind of love you need.

Types of Love:

- *Eros* or Passionate, Sexual. The first kind of love is named after Eros, the Greek god of love and fertility.
- *Philia* or Affectionate. Friendship is often characterized this way.
- *Storge* or Familiar. Such as between parents and children.
- *Agape* or Selfless. This is universal love, such as for strangers, nature or God.
- *Ludus* or Playful. Uncommitted love, flirting.
- *Pragma* or Enduring. Practical, founded on reason or duty.
- *Philautia.* Love of the Self.

I wrote this poem on the occasion of the transition of my soulmate:

Elaine Robnett Moore

Eternal Love

And there were times
 When we were
Enough
 To last
  A thousand
   Lifetimes

Love is eternal.

Elaine Robnett Moore

* Necklace - Rain - Freshwater Pearls, Apatite, Tanzanite, Vermeil

16

You'll Never Love This Way Again

Elaine Robnett Moore

> *"Yes, you can have more than one true love/soulmate in your life. Each one comes into your life for a moment, a season, a lifetime. Cherish the time!"*
> *-erm*

    Hold close the gifts each one brings you. Each gift and giver is uniquely different and original. When the time passes, if it must pass, rejoice in the moments you had. This beautiful human being came into your life not by accident, but on purpose. You may never accept or know what you did to deserve this miracle. What is most amazing is that for whatever reasons, you were chosen, with great care, to receive these blessings.

    All he or she gave you is yours forever. The time you had together could not have been extended no matter your desire. In order for it to be the perfect love, it has to be exactly as you experienced or are experiencing it. Not a second more except in your heart, your soul, and your memories. If you become angry or melancholy because the time has passed, you will lose. Don't be foolish. Rather than lament the loss - cherish the priceless gift your moments together gave you. Hold on to the love, the memories, and the amazingly marvelous perfection of it.

The fact is that each love is so unique, so spectacular that the only thing they have in common with each other, is you. The priceless miracle of it is that what you receive includes beautiful memories tucked safely away in your heart forever more. The passion of that time will play in full color, complete with the touch of your lover's hand, the brush of their lips and the ardor in their eyes, whenever you desire.

One of my favorite memories is of him sitting in a casual setting surrounded by several others listening intently to what he was saying. He was in his element. I was sitting across the room and he looked up, searching for me, making eye contact and in that moment there were only the two of us. In the middle of a crowded room the intimacy of those seconds were so intense, his passion so profound that in that glance, those sweet seconds, he made love to me with his beautiful brown eyes.

"Have enough courage to trust love one more time
and always one more time."
-Maya Angelou

You'll never love this way again.

Elaine Robnett Moore

* Necklace - Alice in Wonderland - Lara LeReveur Polymer Clay, Sterling Silver, Swarovski Crystal, Rubber

17

Once Upon a Time

"Once upon a time, there was you."
-erm

This book would not be complete without this chapter. I wish for everyone, at least once, to have a *Once upon a time* experience.

Once upon a time, when I was young, there was this sweet country boy who lifted me over a backyard fence, took me in his arms, gave me my first kiss, and made my heart skip a beat. Today he still makes me smile.

Once upon a time, there was a prince who flew from India to St. Louis to take me to dinner. He left the next morning going back overseas. His castles were real, his time limited.

Once upon a time, there was a beautiful, gifted, quiet man from Chicago who introduced me to jazz, brought calm to my crazy, joy to my pain and in the end he stole my heart and the music never ends.

Once upon a time, there was a young man who convinced me age was simply a number. In the beginning, I was his mentor.

Somewhere along the way, the tables turned and the lines blurred.

Once upon a time, there was a handsome prince with a sweet smile standing behind me in a queue for a flight to London. He introduced himself. Destiny seated us across the aisle from each other. His laugh was infectious and his stories engaging. London was just the beginning.

Once upon a time, there was a brilliant man who took my breath away, every time he walked into a room, spoke my name, or touched me - with his eyes, his ideas, his dreams, and his soul. Even now, when I speak his name, he takes my breath away, one more time.

Once upon a time...

Elaine Robnett Moore

* Necklace - Abstract Art - Inziza Beads, Chain, Faux Sinew

18

Art Is the Breath of Life

Elaine Robnett Moore

> *"Recognize it. Treasure it. Embrace it.*
> *Enjoy it. Create it. Surround yourself with it."*
> *-erm*

Art is everywhere and everything. The fact that it plays such a crucial role in my life is both a magnificent gift and a daunting responsibility! Art is the way I breathe; it is the rhythm of my soul. I believe, in one way or another, it is the same for all of us. Whether one is a creator, or a connoisseur of art, both are equally important.

Artists will create with or without an audience and with or without financial reward. For many artists the validation of their work stimulates growth.

Each form of one's craft whether visual, physical, audio, written, musical, or virtual, is a fragment of the Universe filtered through a caregiver. The artists' love of the Universe is deep, profound, and creative. They have been chosen to bring forth the colors, the words, the shapes, the movements, the touch, and the sounds of life. No true artist takes responsibility for the finished pieces they create. They are driven, no, compelled, by the energy of ancestors, the Universe, their God, Nature, to allow themselves to be used as conduits. They give permission to this energy, this power, to come through them to produce the creations you experience.

How many times have you heard an artist say that the characters in a book had a mind of their own, that the paint on a canvas took on a life of its own, or, I started out with one design in mind and it became something completely different. Art, in any form, has its own life and its own energy. Savor it. Enjoy it.

If you believe you are not in touch with it, think about this. There are masterpieces all around you that are not man-made. There is the beauty of a spider web, the wonder of rock formations, a rose in bloom, a butterfly, a field of sunflowers, a waterfall, a snowflake, a cactus, an ocean at sunset, a zebra, a tree, a raindrop, a rainbow. Nature is an awesome artist.

What a wonderful gift to be chosen to create, collect, enjoy, and recognize art. Did I mention the peace one experiences stringing beads?

I remember when I first started stringing beads. Someone said to me, "You are an artist." I said, "I am not an artist. I am a business woman and I have no intention of being an artist." I always smile when I think of this exchange as 'famous last words'. Clearly, I had no clue. I think God and my mother have always gotten a kick out of watching me evolve into what they knew from the beginning I would, at some point, have to acknowledge. I am an artist and I share my gifts with those I teach.

Art is the breath of life.

Elaine Robnett Moore

* Necklace - Freedom - Inziza bead, sterling silver, rubber

19

Art Miracles

Elaine Robnett Moore

> *"Stay open...allow art and art miracles*
> *to announce their arrival in your life."*
> *-erm*

Your art, your miracle, may come in any of a thousand forms. Perhaps it is a word of encouragement. It could be the first words you write in the journal you always wanted to start. It could be the perfect repair you executed on an old staircase, or your first attempt to bake a cake. How about your four hundred and forty fourth endeavor to get a song you wrote acknowledged. Stay open. Stay alert. So that no matter how the message comes, you recognize it and embrace your miracle.

Every form of art has purpose. It evokes feelings - bold, subtle, happy, and tearful. The visual arts - paintings, sculpture, jewelry, fiber, graphic, etc. - all use color, texture, shape and shadow. The performing arts of dance, theater and music create the interplay between rhythm and form. The artistry of cooking and baking brings the perfect dish, the sublime flavor on one's tongue, and the aromas that waft through the air. Literary works creatively weave words into the rhythms of poetry, the tapestry of prose.

The art of living as part of nature is gardening, observing nature, flowers, light, shadows, and textures in forms, which change with the seasons and those that remain stable in their enduring beauty.

Every single something is a miracle, here to give us hope, joy, tears, and power. We experience an inner sense of direction, wisdom, validation, self-worth and peace from these many gifts. I have repeatedly said, stay open, accept the gifts the Universe offers, recognize the answers to your prayers, and one of my favorites - recognize the signs you ask for, to confirm you are on the right path. This is especially true if you are an artist searching for your next work of art.

As I write this chapter, I find it difficult to stay focused. What I want to do is dance. I want to dance because this book is one of my miracles. You may ask how did I determine this was one of my miracles? It is simple. While writing each chapter, the topic of the chapter would be brought up by the party I was speaking with, through conversation or serendipitous encounter. Initially, I was surprised and wondered how these people even knew I was writing a book, much less about this specific subject. Eventually, I accepted that it was part of the process for me. The people I encountered knew nothing about my book but they did have information I needed, or came to confirm the topic was to be included. When you consider the sixteen years it took me to complete this book, these encounters were definitely miraculous.

Allow me to introduce you to some of the artists I admire and whose work I consider their miracles. *Joyce Scott is an internationally renowned bead artist who tells a vibrant, raw story through her bead sculptures, often symbolic of the plight of African Americans in the past and present. Her use of imagery and color is authentic, compelling, and sometimes painful. I am completely spellbound by her work.

*Innocent Nkurunziza creates paintings that are bold, captivating abstract depictions of the people, energy and scenes of Rwanda. His ability to integrate unusual materials successfully into his work and maintain its integrity amazes me. I love the mesmerizing effect the people in his paintings have on me. I find his work can, on occasion, be haunting; it is always intriguing. *Hannelore McDaniel weaves beads into necklace tapestries in ways reflective of odd shaped funky paintings that fit sweetly around your neck. They are rich in color, and peppered with bits and pieces of this and that. I am in awe of the look and feel of her work.

*Maya Angelou is an internationally renowned poet whose words speak directly to my soul. This line and title of one of her poems says all that need be said of her, "And still I rise." *Jabari Asim is a prolific writer who never disappoints. He takes you inside the world he reveals or the one he creates. It is always difficult for me to put one of his books down before it's finished.

*Zarmina Said is a couturier whose designs are Paris runway ready. She turns hand woven textiles into divine designs rich in color and style, deliciously elegant. *Bill Kohn is a painter whose dazzling colors and dizzying perspectives, transports me instantly into the center of his work, and their beauty holds me.

*Omi Gray is a textile artist, whose passion is embedded in the work she creates. Her pieces mirror the whimsical side of nature; I am enraptured by the look and feel of her scarves, her wall hangings, and everything she does. The energy she weaves into her pieces takes my breath away.

This list, my list, is never complete. There will be more to come. Create your list.

Art MAGIC.

* Joyce Scott - See Glossary
* Innocent Nkurunziza - See Glossary
* Hannelore McDaniel - See Glossary
* Maya Angelou - See Glossary
* Jabari Asim - See Glossary
* Zarmina Said - See Glossary
* Bill Kohn - See Glossary
* Omi Gray - See Glossary

Elaine Robnett Moore

* *Necklace - Dream Catcher - Bone, Amazonite, Sterling Silver Chain, Eye Lash Yarn, Rubber, Faux Sinew*

20

Dare

Elaine Robnett Moore

> *"'It won't do you any harm, if it doesn't do you any good.'*
> *Apply this to what you are considering,*
> *then go ahead, take a chance."*
> *-Nana*

This quote comes from my Nana, who was an amazing woman way ahead of her time. She was an artist, a pianist who was once, as a teenager, invited to play with the St. Louis Symphony Orchestra. Later, she worked with Scott Joplin as his assistant, helping him compose music (because she was young and Mr. Joplin had a scandalous reputation, her mother always chaperoned her). Nana owned the first African American Dance Studio west of the Mississippi River, taught ballet, tap, pointe and contemporary dance. She was taught by a European ballet master. She also taught typing at Sumner High School in St. Louis, Missouri. She traveled extensively throughout the United States, Mexico, Canada and Cuba.

When I was a young adult, she would say, "It won't do you any harm, if it doesn't do you any good." How profound is that! I consider it the foundation for many of the turns I have taken on my life's journey. She would say, "Think about what you want to do. If it can't harm you then what's to stop you from taking a chance?" This has always helped me to step out there. I love the way it empowers me.

There will be times in life when you want to attempt something new or different. If you hesitate because you are afraid, you may be missing the chance of a lifetime. I offer you these wise words of my Nana that I use as a measure whenever I am faced with these kinds of decisions. If "It won't do you any harm, if it doesn't do you any good" applies, then why not try it? (You may have to read this a few times to understand it). She believed in making things happen, taking chances, and going on adventures.

Thanks to her wisdom, I have gone parasailing in the Bahamas, sailing in the Caribbean, tree walking in Ghana, hiking through a jungle to see orangutans on the island of Borneo, flown in single engine, twin engine and seaplanes. I have written books, met Presidents, (the most memorable was Obama), spent a day with Maya Angelou, dined with princes, helped birth seven babies, taken walks outside during a pandemic and on and on.

Hopefully, my adventures will inspire my children, grands, friends, and others to live life to the fullest. Adventures are memories you will cherish and revisit the rest of your life. What is your next exciting memory going to be?

Dare.

Elaine Robnett Moore

* Necklace - Royal Flush - A. Styles Polymer Clay, Silver, Swarovski Crystal, Rubber

21

Welcome the Challenge

Elaine Robnett Moore

"The more arduous the journey to overcome an obstacle, the greater the gift that awaits you. I have come to believe there is no such thing as difficult, only varying degrees of easy."
- erm

When faced with a challenge, approach it with the knowledge that you have the power and ability to overcome it and to succeed. When presented with an obstacle, change it to an opportunity. By simply changing the word, you have already diminished its negative power. Imagine the gratification of having successfully navigated through, around, over, or under, the obstruction. Appreciate that obstacles are there to be conquered. Remember, the greater the challenge the greater the gift. I have found that challenges are preludes to new beginnings and wonderful gifts. These are rewards from the Universe that we earn by meeting obstacles and defeating them.

The key I use is to approach each challenge as if it's a move on a game board. One of the funniest and most creative methods I figured out to get around an obstacle occurred when I first brought my aunt with Alzheimer's to live with me. I wanted her to be accepted into a daycare program. The facility required an X-ray prior to acceptance into the program. An important thing to remember here is that because of her Alzheimer's she doesn't remember anything current for more than about fifteen minutes.

She refused to go to a doctor's office. So, I found a doctor who would make home visits. (Do you have any idea how difficult this is to do in today's times?) Then, I had the doctor find an X-ray technician who also made home visits.

On the day the technician was due to come, my aunt announced she was not going to have any X-rays, as they were dangerous. I couldn't believe it! Not to be outdone by my stubborn aunt, I called the technician and told him, "When you come today you can be anything you want except an X-ray technician!" He was in shock. He asked, "Who do you want me to be?" I said, "I don't care. You are the expert at X-rays so you will have to figure it out." (It had been a very stressful day for me). I also told him that when I took him to meet her, he should greet her as if they had been friends for years. Rather than acknowledge she doesn't remember you, she will pretend she knows who you are.

When he arrived with the huge portable X-ray machine he greeted her as an old friend. He told her he had always wanted a photo of the two of them, so would she mind sitting and posing with him for the photo. She agreed and smiled. He sat with her and had me pretend to take a picture of them using the X-ray machine. The expression on my aunt's face said she couldn't figure out the machine, but she wasn't going to let us know she didn't recognize it as a camera. He then told her he needed to put a board (the X-ray film) behind her in order for her to be in the right position and did she mind if he took a picture of her by herself. She was flattered.

I won that round with her! He got great X-rays. According to her, to this day she hasn't had an X-ray. That experience became the foundation of finding ways to handle her without confrontation or confusion, just love and creative thinking.

Welcome the challenge.

Elaine Robnett Moore

* Necklace - Purple Rain - Jackie Brazil Resin Beads, Rwanda Paper, Swarovski Crystal

22

Carpe Diem
Seize the Day

Elaine Robnett Moore

"At times I am amazed to find out why I am where I am, when I thought I was there for something else."
-erm

There are many life lessons to illustrate 'carpe diem'. The fact that we have these experiences adds elements of mystery and wonder to our journeys. Here are some that have helped guide me in my life.

I had made exact plans to get together with a specific set of friends. My expectations were set and I believed that meeting those friends was to be the most important part of the evening. In fact, it wasn't. My friends couldn't make it and I was faced with a choice: stay home and lament the loss of the evening, or, go out and be open to discovering why I was going alone and what would be my new experiences.

I went out. I enjoy being on my own. During the course of the evening, I met new people. I realized how much I had gained by being willing to be open to whatever came my way.

I planned to attend a special event. It was a once in a lifetime experience. And at the last minute it was cancelled. Initially, I was extremely disappointed. I stayed home, and received a phone call with an invitation to meet someone who was passing through that very night, and whom I hadn't seen in forever.

And then there was the time I had to get to the grocery store. It was imperative. I needed strawberry ice cream. But, I found out what I really needed was to give some money to the homeless woman standing outside the store.

There was the time I went to the hospital thinking I was there to deliver my baby. What should have been an easy delivery turned into a completely different kind of event. I ended up with serious complications, at one point, running a high fever (104+) and being packed in ice. There was concern that I might not survive.

Let me take you back to my childhood for a moment. All of my life, up until the birth of Charmyn I had been afraid of dying, especially during overcast days in fall and winter months. This fear would cause panic attacks from time to time. Fast forward to the delivery of my fourth child. While running a fever for several days, I experienced seeing the proverbial light at the end of the tunnel that called to me spiritually. I remember having a strong sense of peace and calm and a clear understanding that all was well, that there was nothing to fear after death.

During this period, my husband came to the hospital every day. What is notable about this is that he would argue with me about silly things like, where I put my son Victor's shoes before I left home. Based on how long I had been in the hospital, (by this time it had been two and a half weeks), I thought his behavior was odd. He was not a man to argue over silly or senseless things. In hindsight, I realize it was the only way he could think of to get my attention and keep me from slipping away, to keep me connected here long enough for the doctors to figure out the problem and fix it. Since I am never one to back away from an argument when I believe I am correct, and since I knew he should have known where Victor's shoes were, I stayed present. He did an excellent job of keeping me focused on life. Though it was touch and go for a while, I am still here.

Three things came out of this experience.

1. My beautiful and talented daughter.
2. From that day to this, I have never been afraid of death again. I believe that by going through the pain and difficulty of the medical trauma I experienced, I was given a glimpse of a future journey that promises to be quite special.
3. Although our marriage only lasted a few more years, I have always been grateful to him for caring enough, at that moment, to help me get through that crisis.

I received gifts that day that I will always treasure - my daughter who is a joy to me to this day, and the belief that death is not finite so I need never fear it. And I thought I was there just to give birth to Charmyn.

Seize the moment.

Elaine Robnett Moore

* Necklace - *Aztec* - A. Styles Polymer Clay, Sterling Silver, Rubber, Faux Sinew

23

No Limitations

> *"Argue for your limitations,*
> *and sure enough they're yours."*
> *-Richard Bach*

Accept. No. Limitations. You have the power to decide what you are capable of and what you will allow yourself to achieve. If you believe that you cannot accomplish something then most assuredly, you cannot. Often, we spend forty minutes explaining why we don't have twenty minutes to complete a task.

When asked to take on a task you are not comfortable with, stop, evaluate the situation, and determine what it would take to complete the project. Then, given your skills, realize that you are capable of doing the work. It may be something you have not attempted before, but, with a little homework, you can achieve the goal. What's the fun of going through life never really challenging yourself?

Those who accept no limitations and welcome new challenges are invariably able to accomplish the most. Everyone wants that person who meets challenges directly on their team. When opportunities arise, the person chosen will be the one who met a difficult goal with a positive attitude.

I have been designing jewelry and teaching jewelry making for a number of years. I received an inquiry from a woman who knew I taught jewelry-making globally. She was working on a project that included commissioning a consultant to review the draft of a manual on how to make beaded jewelry for the country of Rwanda. I reported back that the draft was missing important information. I was then asked if I would consider writing the manual. I stated that while I had been teaching for several years, I had never written a manual on beading.

She asked if I could write it. I thought about it and realized it was the opportunity to write the book that I had always wanted to write for my students. While I had never written a book on making and designing jewelry, I was confident that I could. I said yes.

I wrote the first manual for the country of Rwanda on how to make beaded jewelry. Since then, I have written a second book, *The Art of Bead Stringing - Artist to Entrepreneur,* that is now in its second edition, and all because I accepted no limitations.

Accept no limitations.

Elaine Robnett Moore

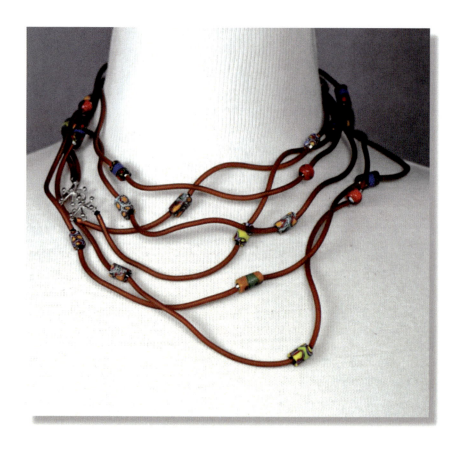

* Necklace - African Candy - African Trade Beads, Vintage Glass, Rubber, Swarovski Crystal, Sterling Silver

24

Recognize the Good

Elaine Robnett Moore

"Something good comes from everything that happens."
-erm

As I started to write this I received a text that said a favorite relative of mine had been diagnosed with a life threatening disease. The question is, do I still believe something good comes from everything? The answer is, absolutely yes! Do I know what that good is, how it will manifest or why? No.

The real question is, why do we think we need all the answers? We don't, you know. What we need to have is faith in whatever our beliefs are. We need faith to know that, when the time is right, we will have the answers.

Let's return back to the good. I believe four things that may start out looking hopeless or sad, are structured to ultimately provide a good ending:

1. We subconsciously choose lessons we want to learn. These subconscious choices become the basis for obstacles or problems we encounter on our journey.

2. Sometimes an obstacle or incident is chosen for us, because there are lessons we need to learn in order to accomplish the goals we have set for ourselves.
3. Once in a while, something put in front of us is to compel us to see that the path we are stubbornly insisting is the right path, is not the best path.
4. If we don't learn the lesson the first time we may have to repeat the lesson until we get it.

What does this have to do with the good that comes from everything? It is the good that comes from each of these challenges that makes us better.

The day I discovered that my husband was having an affair is an excellent example. I thought my life was over. It was as if he had snatched my heart out of my body. That was over forty years ago. It took a couple of years to begin to realize that in fact, it was absolutely the very best thing that could have happened to me. I took back control of my life, as well as the lives of my children. I discovered a whole new beautiful world, full of love, joy, peace, art, and success as a woman and a human being.

Had I stayed in a marriage based on lies, I would never have experienced what real passion and unconditional love truly are. Was the process painful? Yes! Ahh... but the reward was more than I could have imagined!

Recognize the good.

Elaine Robnett Moore

* *Necklace - Round-About - Sterling Silver, Rubber*

25

Let Go, Let God, Let the Universe

"When you have done all you can to resolve a problem, release it, let it go."

This is a difficult thing to do. We say we have faith and that we believe in a higher power. But do we really believe, or do we simply use empty words? Without question, it is hard to practice letting go. We have a tendency to want to stay in control.

The truth is you cannot just talk about having faith. Faith can be defined in different ways. Your faith may be a universal belief that things will work out, or it can be based on a belief in a God or a higher power. If you say the words but do not believe you have the power to cause things to happen, nothing will happen.

When you believe that the energy necessary for you to succeed is within your core being, it is. After you have done all things possible to secure a positive outcome, release your doubts, relax, and let go. Whatever the outcome, it will be exactly what is in your best interest, and on time, even when it looks bad.

When I first started to make jewelry, I had said to myself that as long as I could pay my bills on time, I would continue making jewelry. I felt that the sign that I was supposed to make jewelry would be that I was making enough to support myself in the lifestyle I felt was comfortable.

Early on in the business, it was almost the first of the month and I was terribly short of the funds I needed to pay bills. I had called on all my clients. I put things on sale, checked on possible new avenues of revenue and nothing was working. Finally, on the day before the deadline for a critical bill to be paid, I said the following prayer, "Lord, I've done everything I know to do, to no avail. I'm done; it's on you now. If it's all the same to you, I would appreciate it if you could fix this by tomorrow so I am not in trouble here." The important part of this process is that I had already done all I knew to do.

This was a Friday afternoon about 3 p.m. I did let it go. I was exhausted and not looking forward to the next day. But I was clear; I had done all I could do. I had to let it go. I put the thought aside and did something I could do like fix dinner. Approximately one hour later a client and friend called and asked, "Are you around tomorrow morning? I have some women who are in town for a conference and I want to bring them by your studio. Will that work for you?" They came by that Saturday and when they left all the bills were paid with a bit left over. Remember, the only thing I did differently was to let go.

The solution awaits your trust. I still have to work each time at absolute trust. However, each time I let go, I promise you it works and each time it is a little easier to let go!

Let go, let God, let the Universe.

Elaine Robnett Moore

*Necklace - Shades of Gray - A. Styles Polymer Clay, Swarovski Crystal Pearls, Silver, Rubber

26

His Eye Is on the Sparrow

Elaine Robnett Moore

> *"You are never alone.*
> *In the darkest hour or on the brightest day,*
> *on a desert island or in a crowded room,*
> *you are never alone."*
> *-erm*

Be still for a moment; allow your spirit to come forth. Your spirit is filled with all the love of your ancestors, your family, your friends, those you have helped along the way, those you touched and some you have never known, but have been touched by you. Smile, because you see (don't you?) you are never alone.

A good example of this in my life was Mr. Fudge. When I was pregnant with my daughter Charmyn, I became very ill. I was hospitalized for a total of six weeks, (see Chapter 22). It was a scary, painful, and difficult time for me.

My hospitalization was during baseball's World Series. This is important because, though I am not a sports enthusiast, and was sick enough not to want a television on, I would turn the game on daily. I did this for Mr. Fudge, who was the custodian on the maternity floor. He watched the game while he was cleaning the floor. He talked a lot about how much he enjoyed his job. He loved seeing the babies and their moms and keeping the rooms clean for them. He told me that he and his wife had never been able to have children and seeing the babies gave him joy. He loved baseball and babies. When my daughter was born I was separated from her and put on a different floor in isolation because of an infection I had.

For two weeks everyone who came to see me had to wear a mask, shoe covers, gowns, and gloves and I couldn't hold or see my baby. Mr. Fudge convinced the hospital photographer to take a picture of my daughter everyday. He would come to the floor where I was, put on the entire garb, and give me the latest picture of her each day.

There are no words to explain what those pictures meant to me. That he cared enough to spend his time doing such a selfless thing helped me to heal. Sadly, he died suddenly two weeks after I left the hospital. I will always believe he was an angel put there to help me through a very rough time.

His eye is on the sparrow.

Elaine Robnett Moore

* *Necklace - Licorice - JB Resin, Shell, Sterling Silver, Rubber*

27

Joy Is Sharing

Elaine Robnett Moore

> *"You are given wonderful gifts:*
> *wisdom, talents, and skills.*
> *If you wish to see these grow and blossom,*
> *you must share with others all that you know,*
> *through teaching, mentoring, and encouragement.*
> *Otherwise, just as you were given these gifts,*
> *they can be taken away."*
> *-erm*

The way we grow, the way we enrich our lives, is by sharing. Share who you are, what you know, and share the gifts you have been given. There is truth in the saying, "You have to let go of what you wish most to hold on to." The more you share the richer your Universe becomes.

I find it interesting that often someone will say to me, "You don't teach your students everything you know, do you? Aren't you afraid they will copy your designs?" I do teach my students everything I know. I believe that when you are open and teach correctly, your students will seek and find their own creativity. In exchange, they share with me their enthusiasm, pride in their work, and their sense of empowerment. What I have taught them, hopefully, will guide them and sometimes be the foundation from which they build. Their work will reflect who they are as artists and speak to their own individual creative spirit. As they grow more confident in their artistic talent, they become more aware of whom they are as a person and an artist.

They begin to recognize their own value and power. They begin to share their truth to help those they encounter.

Yes, once in a while someone will copy one of my designs, but my signature or yours is the unique energy that each of us weaves into what we create. No amount of copying can ever duplicate my energy or yours, as it is indelibly a part of who we are and anything we create.

*Innocent Nkurunziza, a gifted artist, came from Kigali, Rwanda to study with me. Each morning upon entering my studio he would quietly ask, "What will you teach me today?" The weight of these words, this question, never leaves me. It reminds me of the importance of sharing all that I know, always. This question does not apply only to teachers. It applies to everyone. Each of us teaches when we share. We teach when we are compassionate, share a hug, a bit of wisdom, or when we laugh together.

Innocent is a young man who could have chosen to tour the city, go out to clubs, etc. Instead, he chose to spend his time in the studio with me maximizing the number of techniques he could take back to other artists as well as a woman's co-op in Kigali. I smile when I think of how many may benefit from lessons I have taught.

When we share, we are often empowering many more than we will ever know. We all are lifted higher because we choose to share.

Joy is sharing.

* *Innocent Nkurunziza - See Glossary*

Elaine Robnett Moore

* Necklace - Tuxedo - Zaneta P. Leather, Glass Pearls, Swarovski Crystal, Rubber

28

Quiet Determination Prevails

Elaine Robnett Moore

> *"In a crisis, stay calm.*
> *Your life and the lives of those around you*
> *may depend on your ability to remain calm.*
> *There will be plenty of time to fall apart later.*
> *You have the power to overcome*
> *all adversities."*
> *-erm*

When I was a child my mother taught me that one must always remain calm in a crisis. To do so is to be able to focus on how to get through the crisis unharmed. This is not always easy to do. It takes staying focused and determined. Remember, you can always fall apart after the crisis is over.

When my children were all under sixteen years of age, I had taken them to Chicago for a family reunion. On the way to one of the events, I had four of my five in my relatively new car, and my aunt Betty Anne was following me with one of my daughters in her very old car. We were on the Dan Ryan Highway at dusk on a weekday going about fifty miles an hour when I realized a car, in my lane, three car lengths in front of me, was not moving. I knew my car was new enough to be able to dodge hitting the car. But my aunt's car would not have the same maneuverability. So as I steered to avoid the stopped car, I kept blowing my horn to get my aunt's attention to warn her of the stopped car on the road. Then I pulled as close to the center divider as possible, stopped, turned on my flashers and waited.

Dancing Out Loud

My aunt did hit the car but not nearly as badly as she would have had I not warned her. I stayed calm and told my children in the car with me that everything was OK, and I needed them to be quiet and stay still. They did. I then checked on my aunt and daughter. Both had minor injuries. I put the driver of the stalled car into my car. My aunt and daughter stayed in her car.

The police were there instantly, as was a huge tow truck that towered over most of the cars on the road. An officer spoke to us on a bullhorn from the cab of the tow truck instructing us to remain in our cars. He wanted us to stay in our cars in the middle of rush hour on the busiest highway in Illinois with speeding cars zipping past us. Did I mention that it was dusk, thus a strong possibility that drivers might not see us before it was too late? I shouted to the officer, that they had to get us off the highway immediately. Then and only then, once removed from the highway, would we provide the information they needed for their reports. After words were shouted back and forth across two lanes of traffic, for what seemed like an eternity, I was able to convince the police they needed to get us off that highway. Reluctantly, they agreed. They turned the tow truck sideways, blocked all lanes of traffic, allowing my car to easily exit and my aunt's car to limp off the highway without incident. The third car had to be towed. Ultimately, we all walked away from an accident that could have been tragic, especially if we had remained exposed on that highway.

Importantly, during that event, by staying calm and focused, I was able to warn my aunt, keep my children calm, and get us all, including the driver of the other car, to safety. That night after it was all over, I could not stop shaking.

Quiet determination prevails.

Elaine Robnett Moore

* Necklace - Evening -Swarovski Crystal, Rubber, Faux Sinew

29

Share Your Wealth

> *"True wealth is love, joy, compassion,
> empathy, friendship, peace.
> The more of these gifts you give
> the more you will receive."*
> *-erm*

When you want to measure your true worth, measure your capacity to love, your ability to experience joy, your compassion for others, your capability to feel empathy, your embrace of deep friendships, and your depth of inner peace. These are your real treasures.

When you do something for others be sure you do it with love. Whether it's taking a friend to the doctor, spending time with someone going through a difficulty, or holding the door for a stranger, do what you do with love. Though you may not know it, there is a huge difference between how you the giver and the one receiving your gift feels when the energy you give off is love and not resentment that you are being inconvenienced. Besides, the task is always so much easier when it is done with love and without any expectation of something in return.

I once needed a surgical procedure. I sent an email to everyone I could think of asking them to send me love, light, and prayers. In addition, I explained that my doctor was insisting that I stay on bed rest for the first month after the surgery, as this would ensure healing with no complications. This meant I would be out of commission for a month or so. My daughter Kai came to stay with me the first week I was home. The day before she left to go home I said I was disappointed because she had not cooked me one of her special meals the whole time she had been there. She took me to the kitchen, opened the refrigerator, and said, "Mom there is no room for another anything. Your friends keep bringing you cooked meals so you won't have to do anything but heat up a plate until you are off bed rest." She further said, "They say you have been there for each of them so now it's your turn."

I have never forgotten the generous acts of kindness just when I needed them. I did not have to fix anything for the entire time I was on bed rest. Their gifts of love did more to help me heal then any medicine I could have taken. Clearly, I am a very wealthy woman!

Share your wealth.

Elaine Robnett Moore

* Necklace -Polka Dots -Wood, Swarovski Crystal, Rubber, Sterling Silver

30

Be Grateful

Elaine Robnett Moore

> *"Question not why something good happens
> or why you receive blessings.
> It isn't necessary for you to have answers to everything.
> Just remember to say thank you."*
> -erm

It is important that we appreciate life's big and small gifts: a sunset, a baby's laughter, a favorite song on the radio, the joy of finishing a task, or simply reading a good book. Be grateful. Note that what is a big gift for me may be a small gift for you and vice versa. Of course, you can include gratitude for such things as, avoiding tsunamis, pandemics, tornados, not being hit by lightning, dodging automobile accidents, and so on. It doesn't matter which. It matters that we recognize the opportunities and gifts we are given every day of our lives. That we realize that every breath we take is a beautiful gift. Say thank you, and be grateful.

I used to be a little jealous of my friends who had huge portraits and photos of their ancestors on their walls. I would wish that I had old family photos to put up. While I had more current pictures of family back to my grands on both sides, my pictures didn't go back far enough for me.

One day, out of the blue (I like this expression), I received a call from my cousin Andrew who said, "I am going to make a trip to see you as I have some things that you should have." He drove down from Chicago, Illinois to St. Louis, Missouri, where I lived at that time, and brought me wonderful mementos of my grandfathers' life amongst which were beautiful old photos of maternal relatives dating back to the 1800s.

That same year I reached out to my cousin Sharon on my father's side and said I wanted to see her when I traveled to Los Angeles, California. I hadn't seen her in several years. She drove two hours so we could reconnect and when she got there she handed me a photo album with pictures of my paternal ancestors dating back to the 1800s that she thought I might like to have!

I had never shared with either of my cousins my desire to have old photos of our family and yet they gave me the one thing I had longed for. It does not matter why they chose times in the same year to generously share the beautiful pictures of our ancestors. What matters is that they did share them with me and I am eternally grateful.

All of these photos have been restored by my good friends *Joan and her husband *Ken, framed in frames from the period they were taken in, and now hang prominently on what I call my ancestors' wall in my living room.

Be grateful.

* *Joan Rosenstein and Ken Roberts - See Glossary*

Elaine Robnett Moore

* Necklace - Outer Space - Baltic Amber, Sterling Silver, Rubber

31

Mindfulness

Elaine Robnett Moore

"You are a spiritual being having a human experience. You are not a human being having a spiritual experience."
-Deepak Chopra

Mindfulness is the practice of maintaining a nonjudgmental state of heightened or complete awareness of one's thoughts, emotions, or experiences on a moment-to-moment basis. Have you ever prayed for something, received it and then wished you hadn't gotten it? Often, we make specific requests, such as "Please let this relationship work out." By now you should know that we don't always recognize what we are really seeking, what is best for us, or how to accomplish our goal. There are lessons we can gain from every situation. These lessons are exactly what we need to learn. While the outcome isn't always what we anticipated, when we examine it, through the lens of mindfulness, it is exactly what we needed.

For example, the relationship was never about the future, it was about the present. It was not about the partner. It was about you, your growth, and your deeper recognition of who you are as a spiritual being. The relationship was a means to an end. Sadly, this does not change the fact that now you have to get yourself out of the mess you created. We should always approach an experience as another opportunity to practice lessons we have already learned or as a way to gain wisdom from the lesson we have just received.

One thing we can do to become more proficient at mindfulness is to practice meditation. Mindfulness and meditation are opposite sides of the same coin. Mindfulness supports and enriches meditation, while meditation nurtures and expands mindfulness.

This can help us reach spiritual goals never dreamed possible. It can lower anxiety levels, add to peace of mind and joy, and heighten our ability to be in the moment. I have found the teachings of Deepak Chopra helpful in creating clarity in the principles and practices of mindfulness, as well as introducing the benefits of meditation.

When praying or creating petitions, we have to do the homework necessary to give substance to our requests. This usually takes the form of laying a foundation that will support our requests. Sixteen years ago I decided to write this book. I put my desire into the Universe in the form of a prayer. It was not until I did my part of the work - wrote the outline, did the research, and collected photographs - that the book began to take shape. At this point you could say, 'Well, you did the work so your prayer to the Universe had nothing to do with your book."

Not so. The part that clearly relates to the request is how each chapter came into being. I would start the chapter and information specific to that chapter would come to me in the form of phone calls, conversations, or a visit from someone who, without any knowledge of what I was doing, would address the chapter topic. Most importantly, inquiries I had made all those years ago began to bear fruit. It is only now that the path I needed to take has fully crystalized. You see, the Universe just needed me to do my part first and to have faith that the rest would be taken care of. It took me sixteen years to 'get it.' Thankfully, if you are reading this, my perseverance and absolute faith has paid off.

To attract the best results, use words in your petitions that will infuse the highest good in all you do, say, or request. Whatever you put energy into should be done with the highest good in mind. This opens the way for gifts and blessings that are in your best interest, some you may not even have thought of. Mindful words use the power you have to enhance the quality of your life and the lives of those around you. The prayer I have found to be the most helpful in my life is this:

> *"I thank you God for life and light, abundant, full and free, for perfect boundless wealth and power, unhampered liberty."*

Practice mindfulness.

Elaine Robnett Moore

* Necklace - Love - Baltic Amber, Wood, Sterling Silver, Rubber

32

Never Burn Bridges

> *"If you force someone into a corner,
> they will come out fighting.
> Always leave an opening so that people
> can acquiesce with their dignity still intact."*
> -erm

Practice being kind, generous, tactful, and mindfully aware of the feelings of others. Sometimes, when one is insulting, rude or unforgiving, it may be because something in their life is causing them stress or pain. Or it could be none of the above. Once again, it doesn't matter why.

This is about how you navigate life. How you handle encounters along life's journey. Diplomacy is a skill we could all use more of.

This is a very small planet and I assure you, you are likely to cross paths with the same people several times in your lifetime. Today it may be in person, through social media, or a third party asking someone if they know you. The response or review the individual offers most likely will be based on how well you handled previous encounters with this person.

Be the bigger person. Take the extra steps to help individuals find a way out that leaves them dignity and allows them to save face. You will be surprised how this can work for you. Remember, it isn't always about who is right or wrong. You can be right, win a battle and still lose the war. Or you can find a way to allow the person to save face, maybe by being quiet or tactful, and you win the war. To the victor belong the spoils!

Take into consideration the role you are playing when working with someone. I once belonged to a professional organization related to my business. There was a man in this group whose issues were beginning to negatively impact the mission of the organization. I was upset by what he was doing, and in a position to confront him in a public setting and embarrass him while ensuring that he would not be able to continue to undermine the work of the group.

Thank goodness my parents taught me better. Instead, I took the person aside, explained in detail the negative impact of his actions, and why they had to cease. To my surprise, he apologized and assured me it was not intentional. He further said that his communication skills needed work and asked that I help him not make the same mistakes again.

As a result of handling the situation in this way, an ugly scene was avoided that could have caused damage to the person, to the group, and to me. The person was grateful and over the years became one of my strongest advocates, though that person did need to be reminded from time to time, so there was not a repeat of the situation!

It was a small price to pay for the harmony within and growth of the organization. The fire was put out without burning down the building or the bridge.

Never burn bridges.

Elaine Robnett Moore

* Necklace - Berries N Cream - Freshwater Pearls, Peridot, Mother of Pearl, Faux Sinew

33

Dare to Dream

> *"Money is not necessary to do the things you wish to do - dreams are. All you desire is possible."*
> *-erm*

When we dare to dream, wondrous things can happen. Dreams are a manifestation of the power we have within our core being. They are our subconscious saying, "Wake up, you can do this."

Recognize them for what they are - a look into your greatest desires - and work at making each one become a reality. There are no free rides in this life. There are always dues that must be paid.

- o Embrace your dreams.
- o Believe that you have the power to make them come true.
- o Determine the steps you need to take to reach your goal.
- o Be creative.
- o There is always a way.

Once you have put your desire into the Universe and are working at making it a reality, it is just a matter of time until you see results.

One of my ongoing objectives is to see as much of the world as possible. I wrote this chapter while on a flight into Doha, Qatar, having just left Kuching, Malaysia. This trip was possible because I worked at another one of my dreams - to create unique jewelry and to empower people, especially women - by teaching jewelry making and micro business development around the world. And so it goes. One dream leads to the next and all are doable. It is important that you realize you are achieving goals you thought unattainable. Once you have the process down, so many of your dreams will become realities that it can be easy to miss recognizing them as your very own.

I used to say I wanted to have a Rolls Royce complete with chauffeur. Eventually, I became part owner of a livery business in another country. It didn't occur to me until years later that my dream had been realized. While we did not have Rolls Royces, we did have Daimlers, and to someone like me, who is not a car enthusiast, the cars look alike. I never drove the Daimlers. We had drivers! The essence of my dream did come true, and what a ride (no pun intended).

You are never too old to dream another dream.

Elaine Robnett Moore

* *Necklace - Rivers - Copper, JB Resin, Gun Metal, Rubber, Swarovski Crystal*

34

Stay Alert

Elaine Robnett Moore

> *"Pay attention to the signs along your path."*
> *-Anonymous*

If doors are open, proceed. If things fall in place, continue. Identify something you can use as a signal you are on the right path. Watch it appear when you have doubts or need to know that everything is OK. When there seem to be too many obstacles, stop, be still, and listen to your spirit. You have the answers; listen for them.

My omen is usually a butterfly. Sometimes, for little things, it is something as simple as an elevator door opening immediately when I push the button. The process for me is this. I raise the question with myself on whether or not I am on the right path about an issue. If I made the right decision, a butterfly will appear. It may be live, a picture of one, a sculpture, a painting, in crystal, color or black and white. It doesn't matter. It is always within a short time of my raising the question. I can be anywhere in the world, in the dead of winter or the height of summer. It is the symbol that reaffirms major decisions. If I don't see it, I will revisit my decision. I will explore other options.

One of my favorite examples is when I had a meeting with a woman who confirmed some very important information for me. I had, for several years, believed that the facts she had confirmed were true. So, I was really excited when she was able to validate what I had intuitively believed.

However, once I was back home and reflecting on the information she had given me, I began to doubt everything. Of course, I started to wonder if she could be mistaken. The next day, I went to see the movie Alice in Wonderland, in 3-D. At the very end of the movie, a huge iridescent blue monarch butterfly flew out toward the audience and me. I laughed all the way home. It was as if the Universe said, "I sent you the proof you needed via the woman you met with and still you doubt your intuition, so if I make this butterfly huge, flying directly into your face, maybe you will believe it now!"

Stay alert.

Elaine Robnett Moore

* Necklace - Moonlight - Shell, Sterling Silver, Swarovski Crystal, Rubber

35

Expect a Miracle

> *"The little big miracles*
> *(the scent of a rose, the taste of an orange,*
> *sunlight on your skin, a bird in flight)*
> *help us recognize the big little miracles*
> *(healing of the sick, protection from danger,*
> *good health)."*
> *-erm*

If you define a miracle as something huge like the parting of the Red Sea or walking on water, you may never see a miracle. But if you recognize miracles as the birth of a baby or the smile of a friend, then your life will be filled with the wonder of awesome miracles.

Let me share with you some of my favorite miracles. You can decide how big they are:

- The births of my children and grandchildren
- The births of my friends' children
- The joy of a rainbow after a really rough day
- The smile of a woman I am teaching when she finds her voice
- The power of a hug from someone who cares
- The love of my grand-babies
- The love of my children
- Perfect words to complete a poem

- The song, *Have I Told You Lately That I Love You*, in a scary moment in Nigeria
- Tears of gratitude for those things that did not happen
- A day spent with Maya Angelou
- The peace of a sunset at sea
- The joy of sunrises in the clouds

Miracles come in all sizes and sometimes at the oddest moments. Everything is a miracle to someone somewhere.

Expect a miracle.

Elaine Robnett Moore

* *Necklace - Khaki - Inziza (Fig Tree Bark), Rwandan Paper, Sterling Silver, Swarovski Crystal, Rubber*

36

Accept Responsibility

Elaine Robnett Moore

> *"Whatever you choose to do in life,*
> *do it with love, peace, joy.*
> *However challenging a task,*
> *once you have chosen it,*
> *do it with love or do not choose it."*
> *-erm*

Responsibilities are interesting at best, challenging at the worst. All of us are called upon to be accountable for a person, an animal, a task, or a project, at some point in our lives. How we handle them often determines in part, how easy it is for us to get through life.

My aunt lived with me for nine years after my mother's passing. She is sweet, kind, and witty, ninety-nine years old as I finish this book, and has Alzheimer's. Aunt Lorraine never married nor had children. So when my children said I should take her from St. Louis, Missouri, to live with me in Silver Spring, Maryland, I knew it made sense. When I thought about it, I was clear that if I was going to bring her to live with me, then it had to be with absolute unconditional love, as love was the only thing that would make it possible for me to handle the demanding times that are part of the disease of Alzheimer's. Love gave me the ability to laugh at the moments when I wanted to cry or on rare occasions felt like walking away. As a result she was never a burden.

One of the things I learned was that people with Alzheimer's become anxious when they can't remember things. They try to hide the fact that often they don't know who they are talking to, what year it is, or what an item is. So I figured out that I could help her when we met someone she should know, I would say to her, "You remember so-and-so don't you?" and she would smile and say, "Elaine of course I know so-and-so!" One day her doctor came by for her monthly check-up and, as usual, asked her the questions she never knew the answers to, like who the current president was and what day and year it was. Without missing a beat, she said, "Elaine keeps all that information for me so she can give you those answers." Another reason life with my aunt was always hilarious.

She was one blessing after another. Accepting this responsibility with love made all the difference. I believe her journey was easier and full of joy. I know my life was enriched in countless ways. The alternative - begrudgingly taking on the responsibility - would have made her a burden and every step of the journey would have been difficult.

Accept responsibility with love.

Elaine Robnett Moore

*Necklace - Sabina's Music II - Freshwater Pearls, Swarovski Crystal, Rubber, Sterling Silver

37

Give What You Would Keep

Elaine Robnett Moore

> *"What goes around, comes around.
> Be sure you are prepared to receive what you give."*
> -erm

How we choose to treat people is most often exactly how we will be treated. If you are kind and generous of spirit, you will attract kindness and generosity. If you are mean and selfish towards others, it is most certainly what you can expect to receive back. In addition, whatever you do with, for, or to others, be sure to do it with a generous spirit. Do what you do because it is the right and a kind thing to do, not because you will get something in return.

Sometimes, what comes back to you may be through a kindness extended to your children, loved ones or dear friends.

I remember when I was a real estate broker, going through a divorce, with five little ones depending on me. It was a difficult time as well as a struggle financially. One of my agents and I were having a conversation when two nuns came to my office collecting for the poor. They asked for anything we could spare. I wasn't sure how I was going to make ends meet that month but I gave the nuns the last ten dollars I had. After they left my agent asked why I gave away the last of my cash. I said it was because the ten dollars would cover more for them than me. Oh, and that I believe you have to give in order to receive.

The next day a check came from a transaction that had long been thought lost. It was enough to make life a little easier for a few months. By the way, the check was huge compared to the ten-dollar donation. Does this mean that the check was a direct result of my having given the donation? I honestly don't know. But it was interesting timing, don't you think?

Give what you would keep.

Elaine Robnett Moore

* *Necklace - Circus - Handblown Glass, Rubber, Faux Sinew*

38

Consider Yourself Hugged

Elaine Robnett Moore

> *"People can tell a lot about you
> by the kind of hugs you give."*
> -erm

Feel the flow of the most powerful, mutually enriching energy on earth - love - as it transfers from the hugger to the hugged and back again. Hugs have an amazingly healing effect.

Twenty-second hugs have been proven to have properties that boost your health, de-stress you, and provide positive energy for both the hugged and the hugger. Over the years, the times I have been most stressed are the times I have reached out to a friend for a hug. I have also used hugs from strangers, children, and babies. Sometimes you have to give or get virtual hugs via phone, text, or mail. Get them any way you can. They all work and the results are amazing. A good hug can cure many ills.

During a difficult period in my life, I met Linda Moore who would become one of my long time closest friends. I was interviewing this really sharp woman for the Danforth Leadership St. Louis program. We talked about opportunities to get ahead professionally and the role of women in the business arena back then. While we did not talk about hugs or the power of them, we did talk about the need for women to support each other in business, especially women of color.

A couple days after that first meeting I received a beautiful notecard from Linda, on the inside she had written, "Consider yourself hugged." It was just what the doctor ordered. At that moment, on that day, it was exactly what I needed. It is one of the most important and powerful hugs I have ever received. It launched a friendship that has spanned several decades and is as vital today as it was then.

During this same period, I was stressed and determined to take the time to come to terms with the divorce process. I was working in real estate, which was male dominated. Being married had worked for me as a buffer. Because I knew I was extremely vulnerable, I didn't want to have to explain or deal with unwanted pressure. In order to ensure this, I only told three of my closest friends I was getting a divorce. Still, what I craved was human touch. So, wherever I went, I greeted everyone by giving him or her a hug. This worked well. No one knew they were helping me through a really rough time - especially the men I encountered. By the time folks began to hear that I was divorced it was a year later and I was more than strong enough to handle the situation with no problem.

Consider yourself hugged.

Elaine Robnett Moore

* *Necklace - Autumn - Handblown Glass, Amazonite, Swarovski Crystal, Copper, Vermeil*

39

Honor Yourself, Release Pain

Elaine Robnett Moore

"Allow no more than a few hours every now and then for depression, anxiety, worry, or concern."
-erm

It is perfectly acceptable to allow a little time to be depressed, anxious, worried, or concerned. The trick is to never allow more than a little bit of time, a few minutes or hours, once in a while, perhaps a day or two at the most, but no more than that, to such negative energy.

The briefer the amounts of time you allow, the better off you are. You have the power to decide how much time you will allow for negative energy or thoughts.

I remember one occasion when I had had an extremely rough week at work. I was feeling very low and a bit depressed. So I called a friend and said "I need you to take me to dinner tonight as I am really feeling depressed and need some cheering up." He said, "I have meetings this evening and am not able to get away but I am more than happy to take you out tomorrow night." I indignantly said, "I have no intention of being depressed tomorrow night as I have too much to do and cannot afford to waste that much time on negative energy." I thanked him anyway and went about the business of releasing the negative and embracing the positive energy around me. The next day was a new day with hope on the horizon.

Honor yourself, release pain.

* Necklace - Avalanche - Agate, Sterling Silver

40

Life Rocks

Elaine Robnett Moore

> *"Life itself is the ultimate high.*
> *Every breath you take,*
> *every dream you dream, every tear you shed,*
> *every smile you share,*
> *every person you embrace."*
> *-erm*

    Because we each have the ability to celebrate our own individual joy and peace, it is important that we pay attention to our goals, aspirations, and dreams. We must carefully protect them as we travel along the path we have chosen for our journey.

    Somehow, I knew this even as a child. The high school I went to was a private parochial school and in the mornings before class, the cook in the cafeteria would make the most delicious oatmeal raisin and chocolate chip cookies. There was always milk and ice cream available to wash it down. I remember many a day when friends would ask, "Don't you want some milk to go with your cookies?" I would then jokingly say that I was high enough on life and did not need the extra stimuli.

    This belief transferred to my adult life. While I would enjoy a glass of wine or a cocktail from time to time, I never indulged in recreational drugs, legal or otherwise, nor overindulged in alcoholic beverages. My position was clear. If I couldn't get high on life, I would have to figure out what was wrong and fix it, not dull it down with drugs of any kind.

Being able to experience life to the fullest, to feel every aspect of it, all around me, all the time, the highs and the lows, the dance all night moments, the quiet sit still times, and the feel of a tear or a flower petal, these are the most profound and greatest highs of all for me!

Life Rocks!

Elaine Robnett Moore

* Necklace - Vintage - A. Styles Polymer Clay, Sterling Silver, Swarovski Crystal, Rubber

41

Words Are Profound Gifts

> *"Listen to those around you.*
> *They have words – the most important of which are*
> *soothing, encouraging, supportive, revealing,*
> *enlightening, laughing, hopeful, exciting,*
> *answering, questioning, thoughtful.*
> *These are the words you have been waiting for."*
> *-erm*

Words are amazing! They have gifts for us - wisdom, joy, pain, answers, and so much more. One can build a nation with words. You can lift a friend or a stranger with a simple hello. You can teach, empower, or liberate a child, a woman, and a man. You can whisper words of endearment and find forever, sing out a truth and change a destiny. You can remember old words that keep you safe and ancestors' words that wrap you in the fiber of their love, their power, and their protection.

Collect words, quotes, and remember who gave them to you - a family member, friend, stranger, ones you found in a book or you wrote yourself. Words that stayed with you and had the most profound effect on your life are the ones you want to keep and cherish.

There are countless words and quotes that have meaning for me, many of which are scattered throughout this book. They are in the titles and the bodies of the chapters. Keep the ones that resonate with you, as they will serve you well. They will be there when you need them. They will remind you of your power, of your wisdom, of your ability to laugh at yourself and most importantly, they will remind you of those who surround you in love, making you almost invincible.

Words often help us through scary situations when we least expect them. I had a secretary who accidentally booked me on a night flight into Nigeria. At that time, flying into Lagos at night was not a good idea. There was a danger of being held up on the road into the city from the airport. When I realized I was going to be arriving at night, I was anxious.

A handler with two vehicles, one SUV to carry me, and a car to carry my luggage, met me at the airport. The thought was that anyone watching arriving passengers would be more likely to attempt to rob the car with the luggage rather than the one with the passengers. My driver put me in the SUV while he sorted out the luggage. He left the radio on to keep me company. In the time it took him to sort out the luggage my anxiety rose. The idea of going out on the road into the city at night was terrifying. It was in that moment of fear, when over the radio in the middle of West Africa, in a dark parking lot, came a song I didn't know existed, with the words I had heard often before my love had passed, "Have I told you lately that I love you?" I relaxed at once. I knew that he was still with me, looking out for me, and I was safe.

To give you more food for thought, know that there is profound communication in silence. When we take time to be silent, to meditate, we hear the words of the Universe and our ancestors. Feeling their council has always helped me.

Elaine Robnett Moore

Keep your words and the quotes that lift you. Listen for them. Refer to them when you need them. They are gifts that have been given to you with love.

Words are profound gifts.

Elaine Robnett Moore

* Necklace - Plum Pudding - JB Resin, Baltic Amber, Gold Tone Metal, Rubber

42

Express Yourself Through Poetry

Elaine Robnett Moore

> *"Poems don't have to rhyme to be beautiful.*
> *Poetry is the rhythm of life, the rhythm of love*
> *expressed in words, your words, if you choose.*
> *Whatever you write will be appreciated*
> *by those who love you."*
> *-erm*

I started writing poetry when I fell in love with a man who lived across the country. I was full of emotion and wanted him to know. I decided to write it down so I could understand what I was feeling. In the beginning (before personal computers and cell phones) I wrote long letters expressing how this awakening within me was manifesting in my life and how he was a major part of it - how I was beginning to experience the world around me in new, bigger wonderful ways.

Before, I had lived in my small sphere with family and friends. While I was aware of the larger global community, I was not as connected as I should have been. But he was global, and bigger than life, and so I began to expand my vision of life, of love, and of me. I learned to explore possibilities, responsibilities and connectedness to not just my little place in time, but to the Universe at large. It was the part of what my parents had taught me that I had neglected.

Eventually, because I had lazy moments, I looked for ways to condense my letters, while still expressing the depths of my feelings and insights. I began to turn long epistles into snapshots of my thoughts that vaguely resembled poetry. I found that I could create rhythm with the words and how I spaced them.

It became a sweet challenge to see if I could capture my feelings and thoughts in just a few words or lines, so that he would understand. He did. He made me promise not to ever throw away the scraps of paper and the match book covers on which I wrote my pearls of wisdom. He said, "One day someone will want to see these." While he departed this life far too soon, I have never forgotten him, nor stopped writing.

I wrote this many years ago and still it is one of my favorite poems:

Elaine Robnett Moore

To the Fifth Color

I have walked
  On the beaches
    Of dreams
Listened
  To the whisper
    Of the trade winds
Seen
  The fifth color
    Of the rainbow
Captured
  The starlight
    Of endless time
Danced
  On the sands
    Of yesterday/tomorrow
And in the wonder
  Of these wonders
I found
  A part   of me
    In you.

            -Elaine Robnett Moore

Express yourself.

Elaine Robnett Moore

* Earrings - Rubber, Sterling Silver, Faux Sinew

43

Think,
Then Speak or Write

*"Words have power,
use them carefully and with respect.
It is easier than having to repair damage done by words
spoken, or emailed, in anger or haste."*
-erm

Words are powerful! Chapter 41 featured words that profoundly affect one in a positive way. Now think about the alternative. One can build a nation or destroy it with words. You can lift a friend or devastate them with a single sentence. You can teach, and empower, or intimidate a child, a woman, and a man. You can whisper an untruth and shatter a life, or sing a truth and celebrate a destiny. You get to choose the words you use. You get to decide the kind of person you want to be.

Think about whether there is a way you can use words to defuse a tense situation. Use words that are kind, generous, compassionate, sensitive, intelligent, and diplomatic. You get to decide which words you use to speak your truth. There is always more than one way to say what is true. Do you choose to be kind or harsh? It is still the same truth. What you say and how you say it matters. Most importantly, your choices speak to the kind of person you are.

I have encountered people who say, "I didn't mean what I said to you the other day. I was upset." I believe people say exactly what they mean whether angry, intoxicated, or caught off guard. I am careful to choose the words I use, and work at never speaking in haste.

My mother, who was gracious, kind, and always diplomatic, had three rules she used when talking to anyone.

- o Rule One: when asked to endorse something you disagree with or do not like, simply say that it is interesting or compelling.

In this way you are not lying but you are not endorsing it either. If my mother met a friend who asked her what she thought of an awful looking dress, my mother would say, "what an interesting design." To this day whenever someone says something I have done, am wearing, or have made is interesting, it makes me smile, as I wonder if they mean interesting in the way my mother would often use it or in the literal sense.

- o Rule Two: if someone is confrontational and raising their voice, lower yours - the only way the other person can hear what you are saying is to lower their voice.
- o Rule Three: never repeat gossip.

Always take your time before speaking or writing. Think about how you would feel if you were on the receiving end of your message. By taking a little time to think it through, you never have to apologize for words spoken in haste.

Think, then speak.

Elaine Robnett Moore

* Necklace - Vintage - Vintage Clay, Batik Bone, Onyx, Sterling Silver

44

Go High

Elaine Robnett Moore

> *"When they go low - we go high."*
> *-Michelle Obama*

By now you know that words play a very heavy role in my world. They can indeed make a huge difference in the outcome of an event, or situation.

Words are tools and how you use them is important. They are your best friends and can change the course of someone's life by inspiring them. Equally, you can diffuse an opponent or adversary with words, while smiling. So choose your words carefully. At the end of any heated exchange, if necessary, you can cut your adversary eloquently, with words. The individual will not know he or she is bleeding, until it is too late for a transfusion (I love this saying). Translated this means they have to stop and figure out what you said before they realize they have been put in their place. Sometimes it isn't the words you use that make a difference. It's the ones you didn't use that put you on top.

The corporation that hired me to handle the leasing and management of the largest black-owned office building in the city of St. Louis, paired me with a business partner. He was not black and had biases. Previously, he had only worked with African Americans and women who he saw as subordinate to him. I had negotiated a contract that made us equal partners. The partnership was put together because the two of us, while evenly matched, brought different skills, skills needed to successfully lease out and manage the building. My primary responsibility was to identify and recruit tenants. He was responsible for overseeing tenant finish (the build out of the space to the specifications of the tenants). I am giving you this background so that you can appreciate the event that took place.

The largest tenant I brought in was the regional office of the Equal Employment Opportunity Commission (EEOC). This agency's primary purpose was to address equality in the workplace. The irony of this should not be lost on you as you read this.

One day my partner and I met with the EEOC team designated to oversee the tenant finish for their space; six of them were women. My partner, sitting at the head of the conference table in the middle of a discussion about the space needs of the different departments of the agency, turned to me and said, "honey, put this list on the board." Every woman in the room stiffened and turned to see how I would respond.

Understand, that at that moment, I stood for every woman in the room and for my daughters who would one day stand in a room like this one. At the same time, it was important I remain professional and keep the meeting focused on the agenda. I could not simply be mad, get upset, or call him on being sexist. So when I turned to him, from across the room I said, with a huge smile on my face, "Of course DEAR, is there anything else I can do to help you?" The women in the room applauded and couldn't stop laughing. My partner looked at me, I smiled, and he shook his head and never again made a sexist statement to me or in front of me. The men in the room had to laugh as well. As the women were leaving the room, they thanked me for validating us all.

When they go low, we go high.

Elaine Robnett Moore

* *Necklace - Red River Crossing - Rock Crystal, A. Styles Polymer Clay, Sterling Silver, Rubber*

45

Truth Triumphs

Elaine Robnett Moore

> *"Truth is always the best policy.*
> *Being truthful speaks to genuinely being the best you can*
> *be, in word and deed. Speak what you know to be true.*
> *When needed, temper truth with kindness."*
> *-erm*

It is easy to say what you think someone wants to hear even when it is not the truth. It is more important to be honest and forthright. There will, however, be times when the kindest thing you can do is to not address a subject when the truth would be harmful, hurtful or just mean.

Sometimes, one pretends to know more about a subject than one actually knows. It isn't easy to admit you are not familiar with a topic when you want people to think of you as informed. Be genuine. Let people know that while you are not familiar with the topic, you are interested in learning more. Folks respect the person who is not afraid to admit what they do not know.

When truth is at the core of your foundation, you never have to remember what lie you told to whom. If, for no other reason then this, stick to the truth. If it is going to be painful, find a way to soften it a bit or dress it up. Always ask yourself if it is necessary for you to share this information or would it be better left unsaid. Whenever possible, find a way to be kind and gentle with the words you use. Truth doesn't always have to be mean or blunt or harsh.

The kinds of truths you can keep to yourself are ones like, "Wow you have really gained weight." Instead, say, "Wow it is so good to see you again." Instead of saying, "That is an ugly dress", say, "Your dress is one of my favorite colors." Those around you will appreciate your diplomacy.

I watched a man I'll call Jack, at a luncheon meeting, give a completely wrong response to a question he was asked about a project he wanted my mentor to fund. No one addressed the error in what he said. After the meeting my mentor asked me what I thought of Jack's proposal. I said I was impressed. He explained to me that Jack's outline contained flaws. When he asked Jack questions that were meant to give him an opportunity to correct, explain or acknowledge that he didn't know the answer, Jack gave answers that clearly indicated he didn't understand the specific requirements of that kind of a project.

I asked why he didn't tell him. He said, "Had Jack said, I am not sure, or I need to check the regulations and will get back to you. I would have scheduled to meet with him again and perhaps agreed to work with him. Because Jack didn't want to admit he didn't know the answer, it makes him a dangerous business partner. He could get us in trouble by not admitting his limitations."

Jack never knew that by not answering the questions honestly, he lost an opportunity to work with a brilliant man on a major project. I, on the other hand, got the lesson.

Truth triumphs.

Elaine Robnett Moore

* *Necklace - Lorraine - Mexican Amber, Carved Lucite, Vermeil, Rubber*

46

Cherish Your Family and Friends

Elaine Robnett Moore

> *"Cherish your family - the one you were born into, your blended family and the one that includes your friends who you have chosen, and who have chosen you. There is no greater measure of who you are than how your families feel about you."*
> *-erm*

There is nothing more valuable to you and your well-being than your family and friends. Keep the ones who love you and are always there for you close. Those that pose a challenge, when it comes to having a productive and comfortable relationship, love them - but at a distance.

Most importantly, family is not always by blood. Often you have friends who are like a mother, father, guardian, brother, sister, aunt, and uncle. Family, blended family, extended family, and friends play an important role in your life. There is always a little drama in families. It makes life interesting. You may have many or just a few. Treasure them. They are there to guide you through rough patches and dance you through the fun times.

Cherish the yin and yang of these relationships. When the phone rings and it is a loved one who wants your advice or just to chat for a few minutes, take the call. Your voice, your words, and caresses, lifts and comforts them. Because of their call, you are lifted by their trust and enveloped in their love.

Acknowledge the gifts each member of your circle brings to the table by being there for one another. The wonderful thing about family and friends is that it is always an honor and a joy to play a meaningful role in each other's life. O, love is so like that.

Cherish your family and friends.

Elaine Robnett Moore

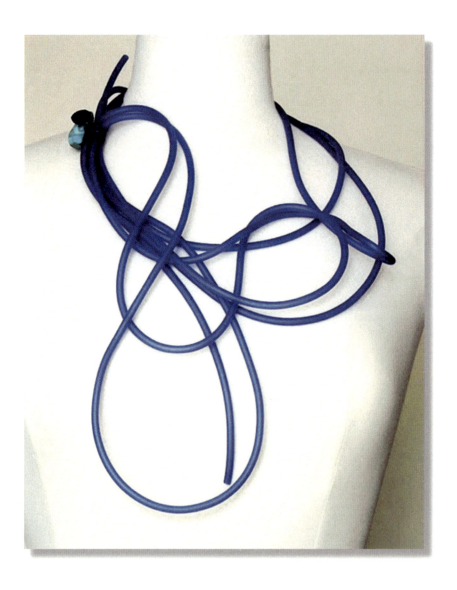

* Necklace - Pathways - Rubber, Glass, Faux Sinew

47

Be Spontaneous

Elaine Robnett Moore

> *"Life is full of surprises.*
> *Sometimes it is good to throw caution to the wind.*
> *Be impulsive and see what awaits you."*
> -erm

Some of the best times of my life have been those that appear to me to be spontaneous! Because we do not plan for these times, neither the Universe, God, nor angels are encumbered with the clutter of our plans. They are free to be creative on our behalf and like any other great masterpiece, it looks like things just happen. These are the memories you will look back on with wonderment.

Always be open to spontaneity. Keep outfits ready for any occasion. When I travel I have casual, after five, and formal clothes. I accomplish this change from casual to formal most often by simply adding the right piece of jewelry, and shoes. I keep my clothes basic so they can go from day to night. I keep my hair manageable at all times as you never know when you are going to have an opportunity to be spontaneous.

When my children were young I used to say I could be ready for a casual event in five minutes and formal in fifteen minutes. If you have children, keep a list of at least three babysitters you can call on at the last minute. Now it takes me a little longer to get ready - fifteen and twenty-five minutes, respectively. Don't allow yourself to get in the way of your next great adventure. Oh, and if your hair isn't cooperating have a stand by hat or scarf ready. With slight variations, these rules apply to men as well as women.

I was invited at the last minute, along with the primary members of a group I accompanied to Accra, Ghana, to be a guest at the official State Guest House. The invitation was for the duration of our stay. As a result, I met the then president, Captain Jerry Rawlings, and as is the custom of his country, I gave him a gift; it was a book of my poetry in appreciation of his hospitality. Because the invitation had been unexpected, I had not been prepared with a gift for a host and my book was the only thing I had with me that made sense. He later went out of his way to let me know he had enjoyed it.

Another time, I was in Chicago for a meeting with Dick Gregory, a civil rights activist, comedian and entrepreneur, and was asked to travel that night with several others, to a meeting in Puerto Vallarta, Mexico. While it was business, it was also fun. The answer, of course, was yes. I always travel with my passport for just such occasions.

Often, I have taken advantage of someone calling at the last minute with tickets, in the best seats, at major events. Those who know me know that I am not offended or insulted when called at the last minute. This is important as it makes folks feel comfortable calling you.

However, you do need to pay attention because there are those who will attempt to take advantage of you, always calling at the last minute. When it is someone you have a romantic interest in who only calls at the last minute, that person is not to be trusted.

When you get a call to do something spontaneous, say yes, and then figure out how you can make it happen. It may be a test. If you say yes to this, the Universe will send you more. Take a chance; enjoy new adventures. You have your cell phone with you. If you take pictures, we can travel with you through your lens!

Be spontaneous.

Elaine Robnett Moore

* Necklace - Sahara - Fossilized Bamboo, Freshwater Pearls, 18k Gold, Vermeil

48

Inner Beauty Is Everlasting

Elaine Robnett Moore

> *"Looks can deceive.*
> *It is the content of a person's character,*
> *that gives them substance, value,*
> *and everlasting beauty."*
> *-erm*

Clouds look soft and gentle, and yet they make for a very bumpy ride – to say nothing of the storms they often precede. Look deeper.

The inner beauty of an individual shines through and gives them a glow, an aura of peace, a kind of joy that, while you cannot physically see it, you do sense it or intuitively know it to be true. Have you been with someone who makes you feel calm and in awe of how wise and grounded they are? Their kindness and generosity is evident in their speech, their actions, and their manners. When they smile it comes from their inner being and shines in their eyes. This is their truth, their strength, and their love of mankind. These are the people we want to be near and remember. They are kind, strong, and generous of spirit. Often they are wise and patient.

We all know of some of those who have met these standards: Nelson Mandela, Mother Teresa, and Barack and Michelle Obama, folks like our grandmothers, grandfathers, favorite aunts, uncles, and those we have met in the course of our lifetimes that exhibit a kind of spiritual elevation. Look for the smile.

On the other hand, have you ever looked at someone that everyone says is physically attractive and you just don't see it? There are reasons for this. It can be that your intuitive self senses deception. What eyes see externally is not what your intuitive sensor is picking up. Their personality may be mean or callous; they may be shallow and unkind. The energy you are sensing is this negativity that the eye doesn't see. Pay attention and be careful. Trust your intuition. Look for the aura.

Inner beauty is everlasting.

Elaine Robnett Moore

* Necklace - Ribbons - Rubber, Magnet

49

Stand Tall

*"One's stature is not measured in inches
but by principles, beliefs and deeds."*
-erm

What do you stand for? What do you believe in? Do you look at the big picture or just one little piece that suits your personal agenda?

Your stature is further measured by your values, and character. We have to move beyond our own backyard and begin to recognize how our backyard connects to our neighbor's, to the community, to the world, and ultimately, to the Universe. What you do with this knowledge quantifies how you stand on the planet.

Do you want respect and status? Then stand for values that will impact your environment in a positive way. Don't be afraid to champion those who are different than you or appear to be different from you. When you speak out against injustice, hate, bigotry, and the things that are destroying our world, you stand tall. To be principled is to set an example for those around you and those coming after you. This makes you treetops above the crowd.

Explore and learn what frightens you. If your beliefs shut out an entire group of people because of their ethnicity, race, religion, sexual orientation, culture, or where they are from, then your own foundation is based on fear and you cannot stand tall. Begin to break down barriers, step out of the shadows, and experience the wonders of inclusion, not bias. Gain the strength of a person who embraces differences.

I was invited to talk to a group of college journalism students, focusing on who I was, what my values and beliefs were, my experience as an African American woman entrepreneur, and finally, to talk about what they should know if they were thinking about becoming entrepreneurs. (See Chapter 8 for a reference to a student who attended this lecture). The students were allowed to ask questions as if they were interviewing me. One of the questions asked was how tall was I. (I was 5'8" tall). Their assignment was to write a paper in the form of an interview.

Their professor gave me copies of the papers they turned in. The single most amazing thing in all their papers was where they described my physical appearance; the average height the forty students gave me was 6'5" tall. For the sake of generations to come...

Stand tall.

Elaine Robnett Moore

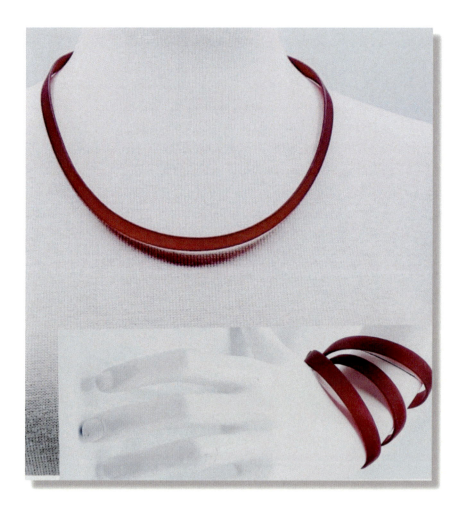

* *Necklace - It's A Wrap - Rubber, Magnet*

50

Get Out of Your Own Way

> *"You must venture out to meet new friends.*
> *Contrary to popular belief,*
> *no one knows how to find you*
> *until they know you exist."*
> *-erm*

Do you desire to meet new friends, perhaps someone special? You have to first take the steps to actually engage with people, to connect with the world around you. Be present. It is one thing to say you don't have many friends or much of a social life. It is another thing to do nothing about it. In this electronic age, you have no excuses. You can literally sit at your kitchen table and engage with others. This can be your step out.

There are hundreds of reasons you can use to avoid connecting with people. You are too tired, have nothing to wear, can't get your hair right, don't have time, too fat, too thin, or too scared. STOP. Get out of your own way. All of these are just excuses - except the last one, which you can work through. Fears of venturing out and possibly becoming vulnerable when actually interacting with others can be overcome.

Please do yourself a favor. Take a chance. Life is too short to waste time being afraid. In Chapter 20, I quote my Nana as saying:

"It won't do you any harm, if it doesn't do you any good."

I know women who swear they are serious about wanting to expand their circle of friends, meet someone special. They know I meet many interesting people, so I have said, "Well, the next time I am going out, I will call and you can go with me. This should ensure that you meet the same people I meet."

Often, when I reach out, I get one or more of the above excuses: "I'm too tired," "I have nothing to wear," "I can't get my hair right," or, "I don't have time." There is an expression that I apply in situations like this: "They are just not serious." Maybe they are a little afraid. I only ask three times and then I stop. I can't make anyone get out of his or her own way.

All of us are timid at one time or another. Think about it this way. If you venture out, don't look for bad behavior. Change the playbook for how you handle issues that come up. The person you meet often has the same fears for the same reasons you do. If the outcome in the past hasn't been what you wanted, why continue to use the same response to an issue. In physics, Newton's third law is: for every action, there is an equal and opposite reaction. If you want a different reaction you have to change your action. You are a smart, caring human being. You can do this. Come on, try...

Get out of your own way.

Elaine Robnett Moore

* Necklace - The Village - Bone, Bronze

51

Be Open,
Be Observant, Listen

*"Each person you meet has a gift for you. Be Open.
Each person you see has a gift for you. Be Observant.
Each person you speak with has a gift for you. Listen."*
-erm

There are countless wonders waiting to be unwrapped by you! Are you ready to receive them? If your door is closed, if you have blinders on, and if your hands are over your ears, you are not in a position to receive anything. Clear away the obstacles. Be open and grateful, so you can recognize the amazing surprises this life has in store for you.

I had a friend who regularly visited a seer to know what her future held. I asked if I could accompany her on one of those visits. She agreed, and the next stage of enlightenment in my life's journey began.

Joe was the seer's name. He told me in my first reading that I had a very open path. If you look at your life as if you are traveling on a road, usually there are many obstacles that block progress. He said my path was pretty clear, which was unusual. This meant that I was open and willing to accept the gifts that awaited me. Instead of him telling me what was ahead for me, he offered to teach me how to use this power, this gift. He told me three things:

1. I didn't need to ask him for answers, because I already had them.
2. He would show me how to recognize and interpret them.
3. We all already have the solutions to issues that come up in our lives.

Most are not comfortable with learning how to receive and understand messages. He did not charge me, nor did he charge anyone for a reading. This mattered to me as it spoke to his authenticity. I followed his teachings and found them to be correct. I may not always want to hear the solutions, but I know they are there. I am sharing this with you because he was right. We do all have answers to the questions that come up in our lives. The answers manifest when we need them. We must work at hearing, understanding and accepting them.

Be open, be observant, listen.

Elaine Robnett Moore

*Necklace - Rocky Road - Resin, Stone, Sterling Silver, Rubber

52

It's OK to Change Your Mind

Elaine Robnett Moore

> *"Clinging to the past is the problem.*
> *Embracing change is the answer."*
> *-Gloria Steinem*

You are the sum of your experience. Seek new experiences. Grow. If your world revolves around your family, a neighborhood, a city, or even a country, your perspective is limited. When you step outside your comfort zone and become a citizen of the world, your world expands into an amazing Universe - one with possibilities beyond your wildest imagination.

Do not be afraid of change. Embrace it. Be open to new ways to look at life. Be prepared for your outlook to change when you are introduced to new ideas, cultures, and beliefs.

It is proof of your inner strength when you can accept, upon receipt of new information, a different understanding or interpretation of what a particular truth is - that what you previously believed to be true, is not. You have the strength to handle change. You have the power to speak to acknowledging that change.

Of course it is difficult to accept that some of the ideas you were raised on are not legitimate. It could be that you find there are better ways to accomplish a goal. The fact that you are open to new ideas or options is a testimony to who you are as a person. Know that you always have the right to change your mind about anything. When you are clear that your call on a given topic is correct, you then have the responsibility to stand your ground.

It's OK to change your mind because of new information, hands on experience, or just because you want to. It is important to know that changing your mind usually speaks to your strengths, not weaknesses. Those who are afraid of change or repercussions from others refuse, in the face of validated information, to accept change.

With knowledge, you grow. By expanding your horizons some of your perceptions will change. Know that changing your mind is your prerogative.

I thought about adding an example of me changing my mind but there are too many times and I couldn't decide which would convey the message best. So I am offering additional quotes I find compelling and on point.

"Surround yourself with people
strong enough to change your mind."
- John Wooden

"You are always free to change your mind
and choose a different future, or a different past."
- Richard Bach

"Don't ever become a prisoner of your own opinion"
- Harvey Fierstein

"God, grant me the serenity
to accept the things I cannot change,
the courage to change the things I can,
and the wisdom to know the difference."
- Reinhold Niebuh

"Those who can't change their minds
can't change anything."
- George Bernard Shaw

It's OK to change your mind.

Elaine Robnett Moore

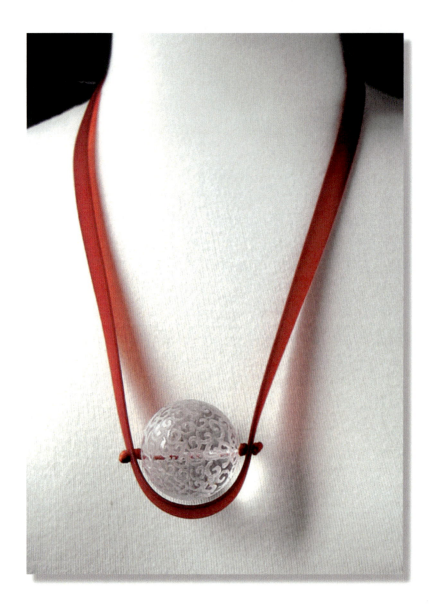

*Necklace - Venus - K. Bachmann Lucite, Rubber, Faux Sinew, Magnet

53

Solitude

> *"To be alone is to be*
> *at peace when you are by yourself.*
> *To be lonely is to not know how to find peace."*
> *-erm*

First, to those who are not comfortable by themselves or are afraid to be alone, it is time to get in touch with who you are. It is time for you to realize that you are a beautiful human being. You are loved and cherished by others. You are worthy of your own love and respect.

If you are not sure, here is a little test. Spend a day or two by yourself. The questions you want to ask yourself are:

- Do you enjoy your time alone?
- Are you comfortable entertaining yourself?
- Are you nervous if you are not talking to someone on the phone or texting?
- Are you anxious and counting the time until someone is there?

If you don't like being alone when you go out, are you careful to make sure you are in the company of others? If the answer to this question is yes, then you have some work to do to get in touch with yourself!

All of us can practice being in touch with our inner self by making a list of the good qualities we have. If you are not already meditating, you may want to begin with a good book or video on meditation. Personally, I find alone time wonderful. That is when I am most creative, reading a good book, writing, or listening to my favorite music and dancing.

Stay in touch with you.

Elaine Robnett Moore

* *Necklace - Midnight - Lapis Lazuli, Australian Opals, Gold Coral, 18k Gold, Rubber*

54

You Reap What You Sow

> *"The energy we send into the world
> is the energy we attract.
> More plainly spoken,
> 'what goes around, comes around.'"*
> *-erm*

Energy is a very interesting thing. We do indeed reap what we sow. Send out positive energy and you attract positive energy. Send out negative energy and you get negative energy. Earlier, I talked about the power of words (Chapter 41). Words and thoughts are energy as well. When you speak, use affirmative words. Use words that give substance to your positive beliefs.

When we are in the presence of people we label as kind, wise, upbeat, genuine, optimistic, gracious, and happy, we are experiencing someone who is sending out positive energy. If a person is consciously expressing positive energy by living an organic life (without negative energy) - one is intentional in their communication, purposely sending out positive energy. If the person automatically communicates positive energy, pay attention. You are either in the presence of someone highly elevated or who was raised on positive energy. In either case, pay attention, listen, and learn.

I am sure we all know this golden rule - Do unto others, as you would have them do unto you. How many of us pay attention? Those who are kind and generous are appreciated and others are kind and generous in return. Those who are nasty and mean spirited are often met with nasty and mean spirited responses. The good news is, if you are not sending out positive energy now and you want to, you can. It is never too late.

As simple as this sounds, when you apply these principles to your life, the results can be awesome. Plant the seeds of what you want to harvest. Realize you have power. You can choose. You can decide what you want to send into the world. The Universe looks at what you send and recognizes what you want back.

For those of you who are saying that you have seen bad things happen to good people, you are right. Let's remember that something good comes from everything. In the worst of times, to find the good we have to rise above the bad.

I practice recognizing blessings and sending out positive energy. I am never disappointed. For instance:

- When my hands are full and a stranger holds the door open,
- When one of my grandchildren says, "I call you because I know you will have something to say that lifts me up and makes me laugh,"
- When an email comes that specifically invites me back to be a guest artist at the one show I really wanted to be invited back to,
- When someone I barely know tells me my words have made a difference in their life.

Elaine Robnett Moore

These are the gifts I receive that lift, comfort, and strengthen me. Positive energy is perfectly timed to come to you when you need it most, whether it be words, deeds, money, or more love. It truly is always on time. Remember...

You reap what you sow.

Elaine Robnett Moore

* *Necklace - Pebbles - Kola Nuts, Swarovski Crystal, Rubber*

55

Protect the Children

Elaine Robnett Moore

*"Children are the laughter, the joy of the Universe.
Love, cherish, and care for them always.
We are their past, they are our future."*
-erm

Lead by example, for this is the best way for them to learn. All children belong to all of us, no matter how they come to us. We have been shown the way by those who have preceded us. It is essential that we do the same for those coming after us. We must shine the light brightly and never waiver in our duty. Failure to give back could be detrimental to our own spirit.

There is truth in the saying, "Each one, teach one." It is imperative that you reach back and take the hand of a young person following in your footsteps. Children make us laugh and cry, anxious and happy, afraid, and so much more. Still, there is not a moment that isn't worth every second of the joy and pain that goes into helping them reach their potential.

We must be especially mindful of their care and well-being when there is divorce, suspected child abuse, and bullying. These are real threats to their physical and psychological health. Children need to know they can count on us to be diligent and proactive in keeping them alive, safe and loved.

This responsibility is not restricted to parents. It applies to all of us: guardians, mothers, fathers, sisters, brothers, aunts, uncles, cousins, big sisters, big brothers, teachers, employers, coaches, mentors, strangers, and any other title applicable to an adult. It really does take a village to raise a child!

Children already have the wisdom of our ancestors and the knowledge of the Universe. We must teach them how to open the door to their souls so that they can access the answers they carry. The better we protect and mentor them, the better prepared they are to lead us. And one way or another, they will one day, lead us.

There are moments when their wisdom gets us through the roughest times. I remember my oldest daughter Chanda, when she was seven, calling me when I was in the hospital. At that point I had been hospitalized in great pain for over three weeks and was really missing my children. She said to me, "Mommy, I miss you everyday." With tears I said, "I miss you, too." She said, "Every day at what exact time do you miss me?" She wanted to know if we were missing each other at the same time everyday! That was all it took for me to stop feeling sorry for myself, to smile, and then laugh at the simplicity and joy in the love of my daughter.

Protect the children.

Elaine Robnett Moore

* Necklace - Fruit Salad - A. Styles Polymer Clay, Sterling Silver, Rubber, Faux Sinew

56

Guardians

Elaine Robnett Moore

> *"It takes a village to raise a child."*
> *-African Proverb*

In all cultures around the world, these words are a part of the bedrock needed to raise a child successfully. Each of us - guardians, mothers, fathers, aunties, uncles, cousins, friends, and sometimes, strangers - are called upon to treat children and young adults with the care and respect we know is necessary for them to grow into healthy, happy human beings. Sometimes we know their parents or guardians, and sometimes we don't. Once again, it doesn't matter - they are children of the world and we must be guardians whenever and wherever needed.

Years ago, a young woman from Kenya and I became friends (Chapter 3). She and my first-born are the same age. So, in the way of older cultures, while we are friends, I am also her elder. When her mother came to visit she said to me, "When my daughter is here she is your daughter. When your children are in Kenya, I am their mother." From that day to this we have been family.

Years later, after she had moved to West Africa, she was here with me for a short stay, and became ill. She was suffering from malaria and had to be hospitalized. It was at a time when I was preparing for a show that was to be held in my studio. Because hospitals here are not accustomed to treating cases of malaria the staff gave her medicine for the wrong strain of the disease. As a result, she went into acute respiratory distress. At this point, I dropped everything and went to stay with her at the hospital until she was out of danger.

A friend of mine suggested that my time could have been better spent in my studio with my show, instead of at the hospital. I explained that she was my daughter; I was her voice until she could speak for herself, and the hospital was exactly where I needed to be. Furthermore, I would hope that if something happened to one of my other children, someone would be there for them.

The night I finally felt it was safe to leave her at the hospital, I went home and found I had an email waiting from my youngest daughter, Kai, who was in a work-study program in Mexico. She stated that while I didn't need to worry because all was well, the night before she had taken ill with stomach issues severe enough that the host mother had taken her to the hospital. Most importantly, the host mother had decided to stay with Kai just in case her Spanish was not good enough and she needed a translator. This mother's kindness was deeply appreciated by my daughter and by me. Her thoughtfulness all those years ago resonates with me to this day.

In my wildest dreams, I would not have figured on such a fast and exact turn of events. I have sometimes wondered what would have happened to my daughter in Mexico had I not chosen to take care of the daughter with me.

I probably don't need to tell you that all ended well for both my girls. One, by my hands in the States, the other, by the hands of another mother stepping in for me in Mexico, and for my Kenyan mother's comfort in knowing her daughter was in good hands. While not nearly as important, the show was a success even without me being present.

It takes a village to raise a child.

Elaine Robnett Moore

* Earrings - Baltic Amber, Gold Tone Metal, Rubber, Faux Sinew

57

Honor Your Guardians

Elaine Robnett Moore

> *"Guardians do the best they can to raise you.*
> *No matter what that turns out to be,*
> *love them anyway."*
> *-erm*

Celebrate your guardians - biological, adopted, or extended family. Here, the word guardian means the individuals who raised you. This could be two parents, a single parent or a designated guardian. They have done the best they could to raise you with as much love as they know how to give.

You may feel their choices were not the ones you would have made. Take the lessons you learned growing up and create and apply the improved version to how you parent or interact with your children or other children you encounter.

The good news here is that were it not for our guardians, you would not be in this place, at this time, on this earth. It is this awesome revelation that is the beginning of why you should be thankful. If they were wonderful, then let them know how much you admire, respect, and appreciate all they have done. Let them know both in words and deeds. I like to think that on some spiritual level your parents are chosen because there were things you needed to learn and they were the perfect people to help you.

Guardians give you the keys to the kingdom, as they know it; use them well. Make your guardians proud. Follow in their footsteps and treat children, yours and others, well. Extend to them the same kind of love and attention you received.

If your guardians were not great, remember, they did the best they could. There are those who, perhaps for reasons of how they were brought up or due to mental illness, should not have had children and were ill equipped to raise them. Again, they did the best they could. This knowledge can assist in enabling you to move past what should have been better and focus on how to use the wisdom you gained from the experience. This is critical to your growth, to your well-being, and to your future.

Think about it, you cannot go back and undo what has already been done. What you have the power to do is refuse to allow negative energy to hold you prisoner. You have the power to stop bad behavior from going forward through you. You have the capacity to put these memories in perspective encasing them in love, forgiveness, and liberating wisdom. With dignity and peace, you can move forward.

Now here is the part that is sometimes difficult to understand or accept when those who raised you had many flaws. It is perfectly all right to love them anyway. You don't have to ignore what was wrong, just realize it was the best they were capable of and love them for trying. This does not mean putting yourself in a situation that allows them to either mentally or physically abuse you. It means you control your interactions while accepting that it is OK to love them while not liking them, and at a distance, if necessary. You don't have to beat yourself up for having feelings for them. Be the person you needed when you were little.

Looking back, I am most grateful for my mother and father, for my grandparents, and extended family. While it was my parents at the core of my foundation, the rest of my family contributed to my well-being.

Everyday, I realize another something that is a direct result of what I was taught. I think about the profound (I do love this word) effect the teachings of my parents had on my life. They taught me to appreciate and respect all cultures and ethnic groups as equals.

We traveled as a family and they encouraged me to travel as an adult. My mother instilled in me an understanding of my right to equal power as a female. My father reinforced my value by loving me as a child, and listening and encouraging me as a young woman in business.

They were both extremely creative spirits who introduced me to the world of art at a young age. They made it seem normal for me to pursue the creative side of myself. There are no words to express my gratitude for this gift.

There were certainly times when I, respectfully, disagreed with them. But, had they not given me the tools necessary to recognize that I could form an opinion on my own and had a right and obligation to defend it, I would never have had the ability to verbalize a difference of opinion.

For this and so much more, I am eternally grateful to Elaine Franklin Robnett and Hugh Vincent Robnett. My love and appreciation is eternal.

Honor your guardians.

Elaine Robnett Moore

* Necklace - Michelle O - Freshwater Pearls, Vintage Glass, 22k Gold, Bronze

58

Sisterhood

Elaine Robnett Moore

> *"Wathint' abafazi, wathint' imbokodo'."*
> *A South African saying from the time of freedom fighters during apartheid, when translated means,*
> *"You strike a woman, you strike a rock."*
> *-a South African freedom cry*

This saying carries as much weight today as it did during apartheid. Women have always had to be strong. We carry our children, run businesses, run our households, protect our families, support our men, support the causes of women, manage to be both parents when we are single parent households, maintain a job or career outside the home, etc., etc., etc.

Women own businesses, have careers, and raise families. They are represented at every level of our social structure. In the absence of our men due to other people's wars, our wars, injustice, his job travel, divorce, our bad choices in men, or whatever the reason, we survive. We don't get sick days, vacations, down time, or 'me time'. We get to acknowledge the necessity of it being all about everybody else most of the time. You do have to make time for yourself, as it is how you stay strong for everyone else. Whatever we have to do to protect our families, our work, our friends, and ourselves we have the power to do it.

A major, major part of being able to cope is the support of our Sistas; women who understand on one level or another what you need, when you need it, and are there with a shoulder, a blanket, a cupcake, their Wonder Woman bracelets to repel bullets, and warrior shield earrings to keep the enemy at bay. Our Sistas are the flowers, the trees in our garden. When we are suffocating from the weight of other people's issues, they provide beauty so we can remember to smile, and oxygen so we can breathe.

Way back in my travel agency days I met a woman named *Maida, who had a secretarial service. Her office was in the same building as mine. She was a single mother of three and I was a single mother of five. It was a match made in heaven. We helped each other as much as possible then and to this day. Let me tell you two stories - one about back then and one more recent.

Maida had a word processor business and transcribed work for her clients. One day she had been working on a contract proposal non-stop for nine plus hours and she had not saved what she was typing. It was Valentine's Day and her friend brought her a dozen red roses. When he walked into her office, he stepped behind her desk to hand her the flowers, accidentally tripped over the cord to the word processor pulling it out of the socket. She lost all the data she had typed that day. I don't think I had ever seen her as down as she was that afternoon. She came to my office in tears. What was needed at that moment was for me to sit and listen to her beat herself up over her mistake. I just listened until she couldn't talk anymore.

While today we laugh about it, it still makes us shiver to think of that much work lost. I helped her pick up the pieces and she went on. She ultimately created an abbreviated version of the proposal sufficient to appease her client. She eventually stopped seeing the friend in part because when she saw him she would flash back to that crazy moment. We Sistas take our work seriously!

The other end of the spectrum is, once, while working in Nigeria in the middle of one night, I got a call from Maida saying "I need you to go to the hospital immediately." Her daughter who was attending American University in Washington, D.C., had taken ill and been rushed to the hospital. Maida was in St. Louis and she wanted me (she thought I was at home in Silver Spring) to get to her daughter until she could get there.

I hated having to tell her that I was on the other side of the world and would be overseas for the next month. She then asked if she could stay at my place until she and the doctors could figure out what she would need to do to help her daughter. I said of course and made the necessary arrangements, assuring her that she should stay as long as she wanted.

She was there for almost a month. I didn't get to see her because I didn't get back until she was gone. She ended up taking her daughter home to recover.

The best news of this story is that her beautiful daughter did recover, finished school, and is doing quite well. Oh, and she speaks Japanese fluently. I love being able to say she speaks Japanese.

There are a bazillion stories like this, some mine, some yours. The point is we are 'Sistas' and we do what we have to do to help and protect each other. Sometimes it's business and sometimes it's personal. Once again, as in other chapters of this book, the details don't matter. We take care of each other, whenever possible.

**There is one story I need your help to finish. In 2006, I created the necklace you see at the beginning of this chapter. I did it as a gift for Michelle Obama. Thus the reason it's name is 'Michelle O.' I did it because of how proud I was and am of all she embodies as a woman. I intended to give it to her even if her husband did not become President, though I was sure he would. I procrastinated and once he became President, I held on to it because I wanted her to be able to keep it after they left the White House. I did not want it to become the property of the federal government. I have reached out several times and have yet to successfully identify the best way to get 'Michelle O' to Mrs. Obama. I have repeatedly refused to sell it because it belongs to her.

My Sistas, I seek your help in completing this task. I humbly ask that if you know of a path that will get her necklace to her, please let me know.

Sisterhood.

* *Maida Coleman - See Glossary*

Elaine Robnett Moore

* *Necklace - Wakanda - Glass, Brass, Swarovski Crystal, Rubber*

59

My Sistas

Elaine Robnett Moore

> *"These are my warrior Sistas.*
> *They are all over the Universe.*
> *Some young, some like fine wine, some ageless,*
> *some for a minute, some for a lifetime,*
> *and some who have transitioned,*
> *who guide and watch over from afar."*
> *-erm*

Linda, RoseMary, Toni, Judy, Chanda, Charmyn, Kai, Vinaida, Carol, Irene, Gibwa, Janessa, Hannelore, Michele, Joan, Penny, Gloria, Terri, Cathy, Catherine, Awour, Maida, Clara, Clara-Grazia, Betty Anne, MaryAnn, Nancy, Kathy, Wendy, Lorraine, Josefa, Dorothy, Peggy, Genevieve, Connie, Malaika, Mary, Liana, Colette, E'dali, Lyn, Linda, Bette, Fran, Vanessa, Natalia, Jacinta, Teressa, Diane, TeAntae, Sara, Dot, Kai, Sharon, Bessie, Adhiambo, Zahra, Chelsey, Chazmyn, Krystle, Alisha, Elisha, Estephania, Claudia, Diane, Deedra, Nancy, Kathy, Juliette, Zarmina, Susan, Suzan, Ellen, Elaine, Leslie, Michele, Janique, Jacinta, Carol, Diana, Carla, Gabrielle, Mildred, Michelle, Brittany, Shannyn, Tiffany, Amiyah, Kalina Elaine, Helen, Joyce, Atim, Kitty, Rose, Bonnie, MaryKay, Ruth, Kamaria, Patricia, Rumby, Achieng, Justine, Gay, Anita, Rashaun, Denise, Juliette, Gonda, Mercedes, Tamekia, Cynthia, Leslye, Tracy, Timia, Lilia, LaCretcia, Koya, Rosemarie, Lara, Banu, Renee, Charlotte, Kathleen, Tammy, Aisha, Lilian, Elizabeth, Sandy, Susanne, Vera...,

No, the last comma is not a mistake. The list is not finished. The expression I use that explains why is, "If I had a memory, I would be a dangerous woman." It is left open for those I have forgotten to list. Additionally, the list is not finished and won't be as long as I am alive. Create your own Warrior Sista list. If you feel so inclined, you may add your name to mine.

Warrior Sista's forever.

Elaine Robnett Moore

* Necklace - African Magic - Sterling Silver, Rubber

60

Brotherhood

Elaine Robnett Moore

> *"These are my warrior Brothers.*
> *They are all over the Universe.*
> *Some young, some like fine wine, some ageless,*
> *some for a minute, some for a lifetime,*
> *and some who have transitioned,*
> *who guide and watch over from afar."*
> *-erm*

Of course there is a Brotherhood for women as well as for men, and vice versa. For the record, a smart woman would never say that no man had ever played a role in her life. If in no other way, she had a father. She knows that men are friends, lovers, husbands, sons, mentors, and teachers.

The men who are the most special and worthy of being mentioned here are the ones who recognize women as their equals and the ones who encourage women to be their highest selves. These are the ones who make it onto the list of my Brotherhood. All are beautiful, strong, courageous, wise, kind, and gifted men.

My Warrior Brothers, I gladly and gratefully list you here:

Richard R, Glenn, Samuel C., Charles, Forriss, Cecil C., Victor R., Shaun, Vaughn, Hugh V, Marcus, Victor Jr., Christian, Etienne, Trey, Emmanuel, Innocent, Terry, Thor, Andrew, Hosea, Eddie, David, Kevin, Bennett, Lance, Samuel T., Andre, Jabari, Rahul, Berkley, Richard F., Paul, Ted, Robert, Thomas,

Jide, James, Bill, Eddy, John B., Biyi, Jackie, William, Ronnie, Johnny, Michael, Raymond, Allen, Kevin, Tyrone, Lad, Etienne, Lonnie, Leon, Theodore, Shaun Jr., Shayne, Leon Jr., Adrian, Landen, John, Jose, Benson, Kaleb, Eric, C.J., Chris, Jose, Sani, Folorunso, Jacque, Darko, Akbar, Harold, Ramsay, Josimar, Olu, Butch…,

Once again, the last comma is not a mistake. The list is not finished.

There are those insecure men, who, by their refusal to recognize the equality of women professionally and personally, have played a role in teaching us how to get around, over, or through them, when necessary. I mention their existence here not by name. They know who they are and I will not give power to their names. Women are stronger for having learned how to overcome these obstacles. That is how to beat the lions in the cave (see Chapter 70).

Create your own Warrior Brothers list. If you feel so inclined you may add your name to mine.

Brotherhood.

Elaine Robnett Moore

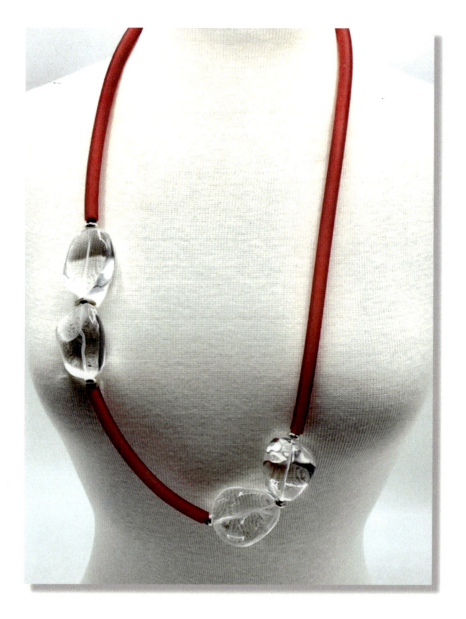

* Necklace - Rock Candy - Rock Crystal, Sterling Silver, Rubber

61

Live Every Adventure

Elaine Robnett Moore

> *"Your life is as full as you allow it to be. Allow it.*
> *Your reality can be as you imagine it. Imagine it.*
> *Your goals are as doable as you believe. Believe it.*
> *Your horizon is as broad as you desire it to be. Desire it."*
> *-erm*

Treat the Universe as your own coloring book. Color it with vibrant, soft, iridescent, bold, gentle, indelible, rich, pastel, and everlasting adventures. Let nothing or no one stop you from traveling the world, setting new goals, embracing your neighbors, celebrating family, hugging friends, challenging yourself, and succeeding at life.

While you may not be able to get to Tokyo this week or Paris next week, you can go across town or virtually visit family and friends. For today, for this week, your family, your friends provide the experiences from which you get energy. Embrace each opportunity. This is the power that will eventually get you to Tokyo.

I've been blessed to have had many adventures. So many to share, so little time! Here are two that remain at the top of my list. I have visited zoos in many cities and seen orangutans often sitting in a corner of a cage looking sad and bored. I always thought they were ugly. A few years ago, I was invited to Kuching, Sarawak on the island of Borneo in Malaysia to teach a master class on jewelry making. I took the opportunity to visit Semenggoh Wildlife Center, an orangutan reserve. In their natural habitat they are some of the most magnificent creatures you have ever seen. They move through the trees with grace, agility and dignity. Had I not traveled to their part of the world I would have gone through life completely oblivious to the wonder of orangutans in motion and in their natural habitat. This remains an indelible, and amazingly beautiful memory.

This adventure also brought the realization that we have to experience first hand the things we are not familiar with in order to fully appreciate them. We cannot look at situations or cultures and assume we understand what we think we see. Out of context, things can appear to be ugly, odd, or unacceptable, when, in its natural surroundings, the same thing is something magnificent and exactly as it should be. Exposure to what is beyond one's backyard is necessary to truly appreciate the everyday wonders of this world.

To put this into perspective, a second adventure that remains at the top of my list is the day I was invited to be on the dais in a Town Hall meeting and had the privilege of meeting President Barack Obama. This was a moment I am thrilled to have had.

I remember the time I went sailing in the Bahamas, from cay to cay. I so love sailing! Oh, and the day I spent with Maya Angelou. All right. No more of my adventures or this book will never be finished.

Live every adventure.

Elaine Robnett Moore

* Necklace - Vintage - Polymer Clay, Hill Tribe Silver, African Vinyl Heishe

62

Celebrate Differences

Elaine Robnett Moore

> *"To truly value each place you visit,
> you must respectfully experience the people,
> the traditions, the food, and the land."*
> *-erm*

The combinations of these elements define culture. The deeper your understanding of the places you go, the greater can be your appreciation. Most importantly, you will refine who you are as a person and a global citizen.

This world is spectacular! If you were to travel domestically and internationally every month for the rest of your life you would barely brush the surface of all there is to see and to learn. Ah, but you will be wise in the ways of enchanting cultures, beliefs, and traditions. Perhaps you will see the hazy blue of the South China Sea at sunset, the dusty clay gray of elephants in the wild, the dazzling white snow caps of Kilimanjaro, the ancient chiseled jungle brown of the Mayan pyramids, the plush emerald greens of the rice paddies in Vietnam, or a monastery veiled in clouds in Tibet.

If you have not traveled outside of the USA, this paragraph is especially for you. My mother taught me these things when I was eleven years old. If you don't already have a passport, get one. Depending on the country you are going to visit, you may need a visa. Be sure to request both at least two months in advance of your travel date.

Determine the customs, traditions, religious beliefs and appropriate attire at your destination. Adapt as necessary so that you do not insult, disrespect or offend the people there. The more you honor their culture and beliefs, the more you will be accepted and the more you will learn.

You are a visitor to their country. They do not have to speak your language. You have to navigate, respectfully, through their culture. One last note - pack light! By the time my mom got through teaching me how to travel I could go around the world with just an overnight carryon! You want comfortable shoes, easy to care for clothes, (three changes can do) first aid items, prescription medication (if you need it), and toiletries. That's about it!

Look at each place you go with fresh eyes and no judgments. If you are in a village, see the unique beauty of village life without the extras you are accustomed to. This does not make them less than those who have more. Do not speak out loud of how poor a place is or how you can't imagine how they survive without...whatever. Until you came, these people were, rightfully, proud of their village and life. Marvel, instead, at how much is accomplished with what they have. Could you do as well? Oh. And don't eat at chain restaurants. Find small ma and pa cafes so you can taste new dishes.

While you are waiting for your passport, why not take a short trip to someplace nearby you haven't been before just to get into practice. Take this excursion before the month is out. Take several of these mini trips to get comfortable with traveling. Then plan and, if necessary, save for your trip abroad.

Choose someplace you have always wanted to go. If there is no one to go with you, then join a tour group. Always check the rating of the tour company and tour leader. Find tour groups composed of a mixture of people from different countries - not just your country. The idea is to experience the diversity of this world. If you are always with those exactly like you, you won't learn or grow. Please don't put off any longer exploring the world.

Wherever you are on this earth, remember to stay open to those around you. Welcome opportunities to get to know your neighbors, associates, and others. Visit local ethnic restaurants, museums, and events that will give you a taste of the wonders of far away places.

Celebrate differences.

Elaine Robnett Moore

* Necklace - Transformation - Polymer Clay, Silk Cocoon, African Amber, Wood, Rubber

63

Grasp Life

Elaine Robnett Moore

> *"Embrace every moment.*
> *Every spectacular, mundane, breathless,*
> *sad, wonderful, scary, awesome, tearful,*
> *joyful second of your Life.."*
> *-erm*

Do you know that:

- Cherry blossoms feel like soft silky satin?
- There is nothing more freeing than sailing the Bahamas from cay to cay on a yacht with friends?
- Palm trees, in a hurricane, bend so far over that their leaves kiss the beach?
- Helping birth your grandchildren takes your breath away?
- In the spring, if you lay under a tree on a windy day, you can see the wind play with the leaves while sunbeams dance among them?
- Your mother allowing you to care for her, when she is older, is a high honor?
- Every day you wake up is a gift?
- Your grandchild seeking your advice is one of life's richest treasures?

Do you know that:

- To enrich in any way possible the lives of others is profoundly fulfilling?
- Empowering women, helping them claim their power, is an ultimate high?
- Tears can be cleansing and joyful?
- Love is universal, speaks every language, permeates all beliefs, is all encompassing, and gives you peace?

Reflect. Count your blessings over and over again. Reach out. Seek with open eyes and an open heart the ways you can love, and the ways you can receive. Now hold on, because you are in for an amazing ride.

Grasp life.

Elaine Robnett Moore

* *Necklace - Peek-a-Boo - Sleeping Beauty Turquoise, Gun Metal, Sterling Silver & Brass*

64

Dance

Elaine Robnett Moore

"Music is magic and dancing is the ultimate drug."
-erm

Anytime day or night, when you cannot contain your joys, or your sorrows, let the rhythms of long ago, today, tomorrow, pulsate through your body. And when it is impossible to contain these rhythms any longer, DANCE! In your bedroom, in the woods, on a dance floor, on the elevator, in the boardroom, in an open field, in the kitchen, in your bed, on a plane, in your head, on a boat, just feel the beat, know the freedom, move your feet, and DANCE.

You can dance alone, with a partner, in a group, with children, even babies, standing, sitting, laying down, in a chair, or upside down if you want. You can dance a waltz, cha-cha, rake & scrape, a two-step, a tango, calypso, soca, polka, reggae, rocksteady, merengue or your own personal made-up dance. There are no limits, no specifics, and no rules. The only requirement is passion in any language, any rhythm, anytime, anywhere. Capture the magic.

DANCE.

Elaine Robnett Moore

* Earrings - Ghana Recycled Glass, Sterling Silver

65

Be Crazy

Elaine Robnett Moore

"Crazy can be cool."
-erm

If being different is crazy, be different anyway. If dancing to music only you can hear is loco, so be it. If being spontaneous is mad, oh well. If the sum of who you are is wild and crazy (I mean this in the nicest way), then for heaven's sake, join me; be wild and crazy.

These terms are often used to label those who do not fit into someone else's idea of 'normal'. See Chapter 5, where I said, "Embrace your own unique individuality." There will be people who think you are odd. Well, what do they mean by 'odd'? And how does it show up to them? If your actions are not life threatening, dangerous, or mean spirited, then carry on. You get to decide what you believe in, the issues you support, what you want to do in your life and who your friends are. In other words, you decide how crazy you want to be.

Should you resolve to be a circus clown or a brain surgeon, an astrophysicist or a hair stylist, stay at home with the children or explore the planet in a hot air balloon, your decisions are your decisions. Only you can judge them. Should you desire to be, for example, a brain surgeon and a circus clown at the same time, as long as you do them consecutively and not concurrently, it is perfectly reasonable and the right kind of loopy.

If you decide to go parasailing, scuba diving, skydiving, or mountain climbing, I will cheer you on. (OK. While I wouldn't sky dive or mountain climb, I will celebrate your choices). These are all good kinds of crazy. On the other hand, if you drive a car without wearing a seat belt, refuse to wear a facemask in public during a pandemic endangering yourself and others, or neglect to study for an important exam, these actions definitely fall under the stupid or deranged category. You do see the difference, right?

I have been called crazy on many occasions, often because I definitely dance to music only I hear and I travel alone to other countries, and sometimes to dangerous places. Let's take a look at the kind of lunatic I am. Yes, I usually travel alone for my business and sometimes just because. Before I travel, I do my homework, take the precautions necessary for me to be safe (once, I had to have guards armed with machine guns). I pay attention to my intuition, confirm that I can trust the people I will be working with and go. On the surface or at a distance it may look like, "Wow! She must be crazy to just step out there like that", when in fact, I have done more to insure my safety than many do when traveling across their own city.

I have always told my children that I was crazy so it was no surprise that one day, when my son Vaughn who was about seven or so, came to me and said, "Momma I almost got in a fight today because a kid at school said you were crazy." I told him I was glad he didn't, because I was crazy. Furthermore, so are all of my children. I wouldn't have it any other way. Who wants boring children? Give me nutty, fun children any day. He looked at me as if I truly did have a screw loose and went on about what he was doing. A couple of weeks later he came to me, with a very serious expression, and said, "Momma, you were right." I said, "About what?" He said, "About being crazy. I have been watching you, and you are crazy."

To show you how mixed up folks can be about how they view a situation, think about this. I was preparing to travel to West Africa to teach jewelry design and finishing techniques. A friend of mine says to me that because there has been some trouble in the country I was going to, maybe I should skip this trip. I thought about it for a second and said, "Let's see, you think I should stay home to be safe. Well right now we have a sniper on the loose here in Washington, D.C., who has killed several people and where I am going there are no snipers. I think I'll take my chances. The way I see it, I am safer there then here." I think maybe my crazy is just fine.

Be crazy.

Elaine Robnett Moore

* Necklace - Bubbles - *Lara LeReveur Polymer Clay, Hill Tribe Silver, Swarovski Crystal, Rubber*

66

Forgive

Elaine Robnett Moore

> *"To err is human, to forgive is divine."*
> *-Alexander Pope*

Once you have mastered the art of forgiving nothing is impossible. This is not always easy, but it is necessary. To forgive is not an option - it is essential to your well-being.

The pain we experience when we have been wronged can warp into anger and resentment. Some may contemplate ways to get back at those they feel have wronged them. The problem with all of the above is that the only person any of these emotions or actions hurt is you. You are the victim when you are feeling injured and planning revenge. However, I was reminded recently that if the act of planning revenge is the only thing you do, (not carry it out), then the act of planning can be extremely creative, fun in a sadistic way, and in the end, therapeutic. This kind of abstract revenge is OK.

I know you have heard this a thousand times. One more won't hurt. Don't give away your power. Don't give your power to those who are not worthy. When you are the victor and not a victim, you do not spend any of your valuable energy on someone who does not add value to you. You are worthy of so much more, especially if you get this lesson.

Not forgiving is one of the hardest things to do. You have to remember to be angry and you have to remember you are not speaking to the person when you run into them. This one is especially hard for me. I have usually already spoken before it occurs to me that I am not speaking to this person, and then it is embarrassing to me that I spoke.

To forgive can be an easy thing to do. This is especially true since you are not wasting your energy on negative tasks. You are setting an example of how to do the correct thing. Most importantly, you have taken back all the power.

On the other side of this coin there will be times when you need to be forgiven. When you make a mistake, and you will - you are human - fix it. Go to the person, apologize and fix it. It is the best way to demonstrate contrition. If there are actions necessary to confirm your contrition then take them. At best it will begin to reestablish trust. At the worst it will show that you are willing to accept responsibility for your actions even if the other person does not accept your apology. To forgive is key to your success, your health, and your peace.

Forgive.

Elaine Robnett Moore

* *Necklace - Study in Crystal - Swarovski Crystal, Sterling Silver*

67

Loss

> *"The time when love hurts.*
> *This is the time it is crucial you hold on to the light;*
> *hold on to memories."*
> *-erm*

The love of a soulmate is enough to last a thousand lifetimes. The Spirit of true love will speak to your heart before your mind can comprehend this wonder. Yes, it is a little scary to open up and be vulnerable, but what would life be without risk.

Only a fool would suggest knowing the pain of another's loss. It is impossible to counsel someone who has experienced the passing of a loved one. The best we can do is to share the things we know to be true and things that may be of help.

- Love is pure positive energy.
- Love never dies. The energy you knew as your loved one is with you always.
- Their essence comes to you in a thousand different ways, every day.
- Your loved one is gone because their mission has been completed. It doesn't matter what age they are when they

leave, their mission here is complete. You have been left behind because you have not completed your mission.
- When you live celebrating the life of one who has preceded you, you keep them alive in your heart, in the world.
- When you keep alive their dreams, their beliefs, the causes they fought for, they guide you and walk with you.

When the love of my life transitioned, I was devastated. I thought I could not go on. He was brilliant, sensitive, kind, generous of spirit, and committed to the civil rights movement. He had fought hard for civil rights and equality until the end. I could not understand why he had to leave? I believed that his mission was so important that I should have been taken instead of him, so that he could carry on. I knew he would have taken care of my children, and the world would have been better with him in it. These were the thoughts I had at the time. But, he and I had talked about what was important, and how promises to continue in whatever way, had to be kept.

All these years later, I realize that while I still miss him, his time here was done. While neither he nor I understood, he had completed his mission here. Interestingly, my time had just begun. He had prepared me for my future. He had given me the tools I needed to carry on.

The amazing truth is that I have a purpose and there is a reason I am here. I still champion all the things he stood and fought for. I have taken his passion, power, and love of life, added my own, and found my purpose. I realize it is why I am here and I know he is pleased. My purpose is not as grand as his, but it is equally important. Every contribution to the well-being of this earth and the people on it, matters. I know now, if

Elaine Robnett Moore

something I do or say improves one person's life or alters their path in a positive way, I am adding value. That one person, perhaps a total stranger, or a grandchild may save the planet or raise the person who does. All that may be needed is a word of encouragement. I am amazed how he encourages me everyday as I focus on designing, teaching, and empowering women. And he lives....

Hold on to the Light.

Elaine Robnett Moore

* Necklace - Vintage - Labradorite, Sterling Silver

68

Be Present

> *"The attention you give to others will be*
> *the attention that comes back to you.*
> *When you are in a conversation*
> *be completely present, in the moment."*
> *- erm*

Being present is monumental. In today's times, it is easy to be distracted. When you grasp the principle of being present, you will be light years ahead of most.

Today, it is not unusual for your cell phone to ring while talking with someone and you interrupt the conversation to answer the call. Be it a phone call or text message, in either case, it is rude and counterproductive to interrupt an ongoing conversation. It is the equivalent of saying that the person you are talking to or the conversation itself is not important enough for you to give your full attention.

When you practice being present you will be amazed at how powerful it is for you as well as the person you are conversing with. Here are steps that can help you have a meaningful and rewarding conversation:

1. Turn off your cell phone.
2. Clear your mind of all thoughts except the topic of conversation.
3. Focus 100% of your attention on what is being said.
4. Take in the meaning of each word.
5. Don't think ahead to what your response will be. Just listen and absorb.
6. Pay no attention to what is going on around you - listen carefully to what is being said.
7. When it is your turn to speak, take a moment to organize your response to what has been conveyed to you.

You will be amazed at how much more you learn and retain when you are completely present in a discussion. The exchange of energy in this kind of a conversation is absolutely wonderful.

Be present.

Elaine Robnett Moore

* Bracelet - Blues - Vintage Lucite Button, Rubber, Faux Sinew

69

Be Focused

"Focus on the task at hand."
-erm

To be focused is to be completely absorbed by the task you are working on. If you are passionate about what you do, this is not hard. When you strive to be the best you can be at whatever you are doing, you will take great pride in your work and your art. There is great joy in having completed a project knowing you have done the best job possible.

Often, you will be responsible for completing several tasks before a deadline. When that is the case, be strategic. Find a way to compartmentalize the jobs. For instance:

- o Determine the approximate amount of time needed to complete a project start to finish.
- o What are reasonable increments of time that will facilitate accomplishing this project in segments?
- o Make and prioritize a list of all the tasks needed to complete a project, factoring in any deadlines that must be met.
- o Make a schedule that reflects all of the above, using a formula similar to this:

- - (Task A) = 8am - 10am,
  - (Task B) = 10am - 1pm,
  - (Task C) = 2pm - 5pm.
- Take a few minutes prior to starting, to clear your head of the previous project.
- Focus only on one task at a time.

In this way, you are giving your undivided attention to each project. You will find that in doing so, it is easier to focus on the specifics of each task. You will experience less stress as you pay attention to the details. This will ensure the quality of each completed project.

This does not mean you will complete each task within the amount of time allocated in only one day, but you will realize progress and success as you work.

My best and current example of this is this book. Keep in mind that I design jewelry, teach jewelry making and design, as well as micro business development, consult on projects overseas, co-chair a bead bazaar, and have grandchildren who often require my undivided attention.

I had put off completing this book for many years because I just couldn't find the time. I was trying to do too many things, and, of course, that doesn't work. I realized I needed to schedule time every day to design jewelry and to work on the book. I gave the mornings to designing and the afternoons and evenings to the book. Everything else I slid in between.

When I use this model, I find myself less stressed, the work is getting done, and I am excited about the whole process. I should have written and read this chapter several years ago!

Be focused.

Elaine Robnett Moore

* Necklace - Links - D. Michele Polymer Clay, Carnelian, Sterling Silver, Rubber

70

Pray for the Lion

Elaine Robnett Moore

"If you see me in the lion's den - pray for the lion."
-erm

Y ou know why? Because if you apply what you have learned so far, from this book and life, the lion is going to need all the help he can get to survive. Once you have accepted your power and wisdom, you are no longer a victim. You are the victor!

Your confidence is evident when you walk across the room. In a discussion, debate, or altercation, you stand your ground. You do this with dignity, decorum, knowledge, and a positive attitude. You recognize your uniqueness as an added advantage. You listen to the concerns of others and look for different ways to resolve issues. You search for strategies to build or mend bridges. If an encounter is not worth your time or is not one you can win, you are completely at ease walking away or acknowledging the advantage of the other party.

During the time I had a travel agency, I organized and handled a large grassroots group convention in Nassau, Bahamas. Those attending came from all over the United States. The sales team at the hotel knew me well, so when a previous group of heads of State from several Caribbean countries did not check out as scheduled, prior to the arrival of my group, the team worked with me to fix the problem. In situations like this, when the hotel is oversold, it will send newcomers with reservations to other hotels. Because they knew me, they worked with me to ensure my entire group was housed at the hotel. They sent all the other new reservations to other properties.

I will always remember one member of the group who had called my office stateside at the last minute and made a reservation. While this should not have been possible, as I had advised the office staff that there were no more rooms, it happened. As the official greeter of the arriving attendees of this convention, I was shocked when he showed up on the doorstep and announced he was with the group. Understand that we had scrambled for every space in the hotel that remotely resembled a guest room, to accommodate the entire group. There was no more space.

This man then said to me (big smile), "Before I check in, I need to know where the nearest bank is because I didn't have time to cash my payroll check before I left Detroit." I reminded him that he was in a foreign country, not the United States, and no bank there would honor his check. He said, "Sure it will. It's from General Motors. Everyone will honor their checks." I am sure, my friends, you all know this is so not true.

This is what being in the lion's den looks like. It appears to be a completely unsolvable problem. At the same time, a man that had already checked into a single room in the hotel walked by. I stopped him and asked him if he had one or two beds in his room. He stated two. Next, I asked him if he would mind having a roommate. He said no, he would not mind. Last, I asked him if he would accept this other man's payroll check as payment and give back to him the difference between the cost of his share of the room and the amount of the payroll check. Again he said yes. Problem solved. See how a little critical thinking turns the lion into a kitten?

Pray for the lion.

Elaine Robnett Moore

* *Necklace - Golden Sea - Ammonite Fossil, Gold Coral, Freshwater Pearls, 22k Gold, Bronze*

71

Passion

"Find your passion. Discover what turns your world upside down and backwards in the best way."
-erm

Each of us should be passionate about someone or something. It doesn't matter whether it is sweeping floors or orchestrating sweeping changes in the law, someone with dreamy eyes or one who dreams, designing jewelry or designing buildings, raising children or crops, saving your neighborhood or saving your neighbor, rescuing people from catastrophic disasters or animals from permanent extinction. Anyone and everything that adds to your well-being, the well-being of others, and our planet, is equally important.

You will know when you are passionate about what you do. It's the one thing that you can't leave until it is exactly right. It doesn't matter what others think, only that you are satisfied it is as perfect as you can make it. I design jewelry. When I am not able to design for one reason or another I am not happy. I become anxious to get back to designing. There are two things people say most often about my jewelry. First, that they are drawn to it and feel compelled to touch it. Second, that they can see and feel the love I put into making it. What they are experiencing is the result of my passion for my work.

Recently I met Mark, a skycap (the person who helps with luggage at an airport) in Atlanta, Georgia. I had injured my foot and needed to use a wheelchair to get from point to point. We talked as he expertly navigated around bustling crowds in the hectic airport. He talked about how much he loved what he does, how he left a higher paying position to do this work because of the joy he experiences helping and interacting with people from all over the world.

Going through airports in normal circumstances is difficult and made more complicated when you are at the mercy of someone pushing you in a wheelchair. Mark was knowledgeable and engaging, which took the stress out of the process. He had chosen to do what he was passionate about and, as a result, I received the gift of his joy.

So, I leave this chapter to you. Fill it in. You have the tools. Write your truth. It is your passion that must be written here, not mine...

Write your passion.

Elaine Robnett Moore

* *Necklace - Springtime - Vintage Glass, Freshwater Pearls, Swarovski Crystal, Rubber*

72

Embrace Your Idiosyncrasies

Elaine Robnett Moore

> *"The things you may label as idiosyncrasies are the things that make you distinctive, quirky."*
> *-erm*

Your idiosyncrasies make you unique, creative, amazing, and yes, a bit quirky. These are the qualities that add color and depth to your character. What, in another, is a whispery pink, in you, is smoking fuchsia. When some are a cool blue, you rock a solid indigo. This, in part, is what makes you, you, and me, me. How delightfully colorful this makes you. Certainly, it contributes to your awesomeness and explains how your very presence adds to the beauty of this planet.

If you think I am talking only about myself, let me assure you, I absolutely am talking specifically to you. This world is a wondrous place, and as you are here, alive on this earth, at this moment, then you are an integral part of its wonders. No matter how small or big your role, it is exactly what is needed to complete the perfection of this world.

After all, a minute would not exist without exactly sixty seconds. But for one missing second, and you would have no minute. Look at it this way: for lack of a second, you have no minute. For lack of a minute, you have no hour. For lack of an hour, you have no day. For lack of a day, you have no week…and on it goes. Recognize that you are a 'second.' Now, do you see how important your contribution is to the bigger picture?

Embrace the wonder of who you really are. Grasp all the bits and pieces that give your character unique colors, that cause you to shine and make you interesting.

Let me share one of my own idiosyncrasies: I have mugs I have collected from different places and every day when I get ready for a cup of coffee or tea I decide which cup best suits my mood, or supports what I want to accomplish that day (it may be the color). If it's a cloudy day, I usually want a bright, sunny mug. Where it is from matters. When I wish I were on an island, I pick one from an exotic place I have been to, or wish to go. Who gave it to me can be important. These mugs have sentimental value, like the one with musical notes that makes me think of my Aunt Lorraine. It can be how the pattern on the mug fits in with what I am going to be doing. For instance, if I am writing, I may choose one that feels scholarly to me. All in all, I choose the mug best suited to supporting my mood or goal.

But perhaps the thing most would associate with me is color and how I apply it whether creating jewelry, or writing a poem. I love color and I am told it is evident in everything I do. Certain people may think my reds, oranges, greens and blues are a bit much. To them, I appear a bit loud. I do my colors anyway. From time to time, a client will come up to me wearing something colorful I made and tell me these colors make her happy. Or, someone will read a piece I wrote and thank me for

Elaine Robnett Moore

the insight into the emerald green of the rainforest in Borneo. I celebrate my quirky ways and share my magnificent colors!

Embrace your idiosyncrasies.

Elaine Robnett Moore

* Necklace - Sea Shells - Bronze, Couch Shell, Rubber

73

10 Degrees of Easy

Elaine Robnett Moore

"No more difficult; just varying degrees of easy."
-erm

Difficult is an extremely overused negative word. It tends to, by its use alone, change a doable task into a next to impossible one. I find it not applicable most of the time. If we do not use this word or words like it that are meant to block our path to success, what happens? We have to find new ways to describe the process of conquering obstacles obstructing our progress and new words that support our talents.

I propose we use varying 'Degrees of Easy 1 – 10' instead. I believe by using this system, you are likely to find no task impossible. The scale of 1 through 10 could rank as follows:

- Easy 1 — A breath away from being super easy!
- Easy 2 - 4 — Not too bothersome at all!
- Easy 5 - 8 — Really, is this a test?
- Easy 9 -10 — This could be fun; it is definitely a challenge worthy of my skills.

This way, when you are sizing up a project you are considering taking on, it would look like this: crossing the Sahara Desert on camelback is going to be an Easy 10, while getting across town during rush hour traffic in your car, is only an Easy 3. Completing the seven-hour project your boss gave you at 11 a.m., by 5 p.m. is clearly an Easy 8, because if anyone can work a miracle, certainly it is you.

There is always the perspective one has, to be considered, when deciding on the ranking of a given project. Take, for instance, giving birth. You see, it all depends on one's viewpoint. For instance, when seen through the eyes of the doctor it, may be an Easy 1 or 2. Viewed with the father's fear for his wife and unborn child, let's say it might be an Easy 7 or 8. However, it is the mother's conviction, after being in labor for 15 hours that it would be insane to rank this at anything less than an Easy 75+!

In fact, the idea of relabeling challenges, as shown, may be sufficient to deescalate the drama and unnecessary anxiety that builds when you take on an already complicated situation.

Should this system (Degrees of Easy 1 - 10) not work for you, be creative, devise your own. You have power and words in your vocabulary that will work for you. Fix it. I believe the only thing left to say here is, "You've got this!"

10 Degrees of Easy.

Elaine Robnett Moore

* Necklace - Jade - Jade, 22k Gold, Rubber

74

Be Enlightened

Elaine Robnett Moore

> *"The Universe is alive!*
> *Everything in it has life.*
> *Feel the energy of this precious earth in a stone,*
> *a flower, a raging river, a sunset!"*
> *-erm*

To be enlightened is to be in touch with your spiritual self and aligned with the Universe. You are a part of all that is around you. When you focus on the beauty of the flowers, you become aware of their scents. Summer breezes get your attention as they caress your face. You are sensitive to the music of spring waters cascading over rocks.

If you are not sure, sit down, be quiet, and meditate. Position an object in front of you. Focus all of your attention on the object. Look at its color or the pattern of color. Is it opaque or translucent? What is it made of? What is its size? Think about what it is used for. Is it manufactured or handmade? What does it feel like? Is it soft, hard, smooth or rough? The point is to give your undivided attention to the task at hand. Appreciate all that you see and feel regarding the object you are contemplating. Try this with the same object three different times. See if there are new aspects of it the second and third time that you hadn't noticed the first time. This will heighten your ability to see what is around you with new eyes.

According to *Vedanta, there are two indications of enlightenment, two indications that a transformation is taking place within you toward a higher consciousness. The first is that you stop worrying. Things don't bother you anymore. You become light-hearted and full of joy. The second is that you encounter more and more meaningful coincidences in your life, more and more synchronicities. And this accelerates to the point where you actually experience the miraculous, meaningful coincidences, synchronicities, or validations. A rose by any other name is still a rose. I knew it was the right time to finish this book.

I knew this because every chapter I had written received validation on the day I was writing it. Not in vague references, but as specific as it could possibly get. At first, I thought it was a nice kind of pat on the back that I should keep going. However, as it kept occurring over and over again, I realized it was the Universe saying, "What are you waiting for? The world is ready for your book today." Please be clear, 'the world' in this context means those who are ready to receive it. It could be as few as one or as many as a bazillion. It doesn't matter. In fact, the one may just be me. What is important is that there is the one who is waiting and I had to finish it for that one.

When I think about what I do, other than the book, I realize how blessed I am. When I am designing jewelry, I can look at the same beads I have seen and worked with a hundred different times. Still, each time I see something new, something remarkably unique I want to emphasize, or to present in a different way.

Every sunset takes my breath away. Every wave hitting a beach is magical. The song of a bird makes me smile. The shapes of huge rocks stacked in precarious ways in Ghana, as if they were the building blocks of a giant toddler, these are the things that remind me there are miracles everywhere. Did I mention the magic of butterflies? Everyday is new and so is every experience no matter how many times I have encountered it. Enjoy.

Be enlightened.

* Vedanta - See Glossary

*Necklace - Vintage - Wood, Copper, Faux Sinew, Leather

75

Carry On

Elaine Robnett Moore

> *"There are times when all seems lost or terribly disappointing. The good news is, this too will pass. It is these times when the most crucial thing you can do is - Carry On."*
> *-erm*

You are the captain of your ship. Unless you are prepared to go down with the ship, I suggest you get all hands on deck, bail water, row, and send up flares. This translates into assessing the problem and determining the solution. Better yet, always, always, always have plan B and C in place. This way, you are ready to pick up the pieces and carry on.

In real estate, one way success is measured is by closing transactions. Every now and then you lose a transaction (fail to close it), be it small or large. The day after I received notice that I had just lost the bid on a major project, I honored a commitment to speak to a group of fifth and sixth graders. I was not happy, and a bit distracted, as I had counted on the project to carry my company through a rough economic period.

That said, a commitment is a commitment, so I was talking to these children about what it was like to own your own business. The teacher had prepared the children so that they had questions to ask me. One little boy raised his hand and asked me what was bad about owning your own business. It was a good question. However, at that moment, having lost a huge contract the day before, the answer was not appropriate for this age group, so I took into consideration the ages of the children, and gave them an answer I thought they would understand and one that would not scare them away from becoming entrepreneurs. I told them that you don't get to take vacations. A little girl, not to be outdone, asked what was good about owning your own business. Again, at that moment, I could think of nothing good about it. However, looking at the excited faces in front of me I said. You get to decide it's OK not to have a vacation. Trust me there are days when that's as good as it gets.

I always think about this presentation when I see nothing good ahead, because the next week made up for the loss of that project ten fold. I hadn't seen it coming. This just goes to prove two things: something good is always over the horizon, and the thing you have to do is...

Carry on.

Elaine Robnett Moore

* *Necklace - Chains - Lucite, Polymer Clay, Sterling Silver*

76

The Elephant in the Room

Elaine Robnett Moore

> *"The definition of racism:*
> *Power, prejudice and privilege exercised by whites*
> *over people of color thereby denying people of color access*
> *to goods, opportunities, and services."*
> *- Cathy Royal, PhD*

I am grateful for the timing of this book. It has afforded me the opportunity to address many issues important to those attempting to navigate life journeys. However, before it went to press, I was reminded of the elephant in the room, systemic racism. It is the ongoing threat to humanity that black and brown people have endured for over four hundred years. We can no longer ignore it, pretend it is under control, or act as if it no longer exists. It is an insidious evil we people of color and white people have grown too accustomed to. The recent tragedies of *George Floyd (a black man) being killed by a white police officer on camera, with such disdain, and *Breonna Taylor (a black woman) being killed by police while sleeping in her bed, have finally caused a tipping point in our society.

The time to fix this injustice is now.

The wounds these horrors and other deaths of innocent people of color at the hands of corrupt and racist white police, all happening within days of each other, have reminded me of how, as a black mother, I have absorbed this insidious hate-driven poison. And, like most of us, feared the outcome of it on our children.

While white mothers teach their sons and daughters how to drive safely and how to put on lipstick, black and brown mothers have to give our children (especially the boys) 'the talk'. The talk includes things like how to behave so that they do not attract the attention of the police. It describes how not to wear hoodies pulled up over their heads after dark. And how, when they are stopped (and they will be…for being black), they must do what they are told and try not to appear 'threatening' (not that this works). This talk and all the other things we do to protect and save our children and ourselves, has become almost a reflex. Until Mr. Floyd's death, I had forgotten how automatic and pervasive our worry is. Every time our males - sons, grandsons, nephews, husbands, fathers, all - step out of our doors, until they are back home safe, it is there. This elephant never leaves the room. It is always by the door.

I have experienced the ignorance of racism first hand too many times to count. Sometimes having to defend my children, sometimes myself, and often having to share with others how to dodge a bullet, whether literal or metaphoric. When you have the added burden of determining whether a given incident is racist or because an individual has other issues, you *Just. Get. Tired.*

Once, my daughter, Charmyn, was going by The Black Repertory Theater in St. Louis, Missouri. She was sixteen and driving the car I had brought for my teenagers. She had my oldest grandson and his mother in the car with her.

Charmyn volunteered as a make-up artist at the theater and was going to pick up her make up kit from the theater. The theater was on the black side of town and one doesn't see many whites there. When she came out of the building she got in her car and was suddenly surrounded by several white men, one wearing a cowboy hat, shouting with guns out, pointed at my daughter Charmyn, my two-year-old grandson Shaun, and Diane, his mother. The baby was screaming. Charmyn and Diane were so traumatized they had their heads down thinking that these men were probably members of the Ku Klux Klan and were going to kill them. Thank God Charmyn hadn't had time to lock her door or this could have ended very differently.

Because the door was not locked, one of the men opened it and instructed the girls and baby to get out of the car. Having no choice, they did. You should know that at this point the men had not identified themselves as officers of the law.

They were told to sit on the curb while the men, who turned out to be Drug Enforcement Agency (DEA) officers, searched the car. They were looking for drugs. Someone they were following had gone into the theater with a package and Charmyn had come out carrying her make-up kit. Needless to say, there were no drugs. The cowboy then said to my daughter, "This time you can leave, but next time we'll get you." When Charmyn got home (there were no cell phones then) she was still shaking and crying. She is 5'11" tall and she sat on my lap (I am 5'8" tall) because she was that frightened.

Since I was involved as a businesswoman in the city, I called the Police Commissioner who assured me these were not members of the St. Louis, Missouri Police Department. He did some research then called me back to tell me it was a DEA operation. I was able to get in touch with the regional head of the DEA and, ultimately, he came and personally apologized to Charmyn, Diane, and Shaun for the arrogance of the men to have said, "We will get you next time", (because they clearly assumed all black people do drugs), for how they were treated, for the officers not properly identifying themselves, and for unnecessarily endangering my family. The reason this ended with apologies was because the police commissioner and the director of the DEA office were both black and I was an active member in the community and known to them. Had it been otherwise, no apologies would have been given. In addition, had the girls been boys, this ordeal very likely may have ended tragically.

No one should have to live with this fear.

There are many ways in which systemic racism rears its ugly head - in the work place, the education system, medical services, the judicial system, housing, or shopping, - in other words, in all aspects of everyday life. No one person of color is exempt, no matter his or her economic, social, or celebrity status. And, NO, unless you are black or brown, you cannot and do not understand how racism feels.

It is not necessary to understand first hand how it feels in order to take part in correcting this injustice. You can be a part of the solution. It is past time for whites to have to have uncomfortable talks with each other as well as with people of color. While you may not be a conscious racist, if you are not standing up against racists when there are no people of color in the room, then you are part of the problem and not the solution. We have to come together and take the steps together to change, remove, and erase the laws, practices, and policies that prevent equality from flourishing.

I believe systemic racism does present an opportunity for people - white, and of color - to open up, recognize the powers we have, and acknowledge the truth. Use these truths to take control of a system that has failed humankind, and be a part of a solution that saves us from this insidious evil - systemic racism. Black Lives Matter.

No more elephants in the room.

* *George Floyd - See Glossary*
* *Breonna Taylor - See Glossary*

Elaine Robnett Moore

* Necklace - Deco - Sleeping Beauty Turquoise, JB Resin, Sterling Silver, Rubber

77

Getting a Hold on Our Humanity

Elaine Robnett Moore

> *"We are a resilient species, we humans.*
> *We have powers. Some powers we have ignored.*
> *Some we have yet to discover.*
> *Combined, these powers, should we choose to use them,*
> *can provide the wisdom and knowledge*
> *to get us through anything."*
> *-erm*

During the course of my writing this book, we citizens of the world have faced three pandemics, several tsunamis, countless earthquakes, hurricanes, tornados, floods, fires, blizzards, volcano eruptions, and so much more. Initially, I thought this chapter was to acknowledge the presence of *COVID-19 and reaffirm that just as there are chapters here designed to help you power through the kinds of disasters written above, the same chapters will work regarding this disease as well. We have the power.

Imagine my surprise, when I looked at the horrific, (longer than I would have ever thought), list of disasters and diseases we have dealt with over only sixteen years. Think about this. Clearly, I have survived and I did so, using in part, the wisdom I have collected and written about within the covers of this book.

I believe COVID-19 is an opportunity for us to be open, pay attention to the powers we have, and see the truth of these words. Use them to take control of a system that has failed humankind, and be a part of a solution that saves us from COVID-19 and more.

I think Chapter 26 is important as we realize that with this disease, a major concern is that we often cannot be with loved ones to help them transition. Whatever your belief system or your faith, we never walk alone. I believe that when it is time for us to cross over, there is always someone there to hold our hand and guide us.

To put things in perspective, consider this. The devastation of COVID -19 is a current and long-term catastrophe. It is the worst and fastest spreading contagion we have had to face in our lifetimes. However, let's take time to look at some of the man-made disasters that have taken place on our planet in only the last sixteen years. How many of these have we turned a blind eye to wars, genocides, human tariffing, starvation, famines, global warming, ethnic cleansings, domestic abuse, racism, economic recessions, neglect, etc. We begin to see that there is much work to do. COVID-19, while cataclysmic, is not insurmountable. It is a killer, but we are warriors of light.

I spoke of the wonder and beauty of this planet and what we should do to actively participate in the saving of our only home, Earth. Remember when I talked about running out of time? Well COVID-19 is what that looks like. In less than six months, life as we know it has changed.

Do you hear Mother Nature saying, "I have tried to get your attention and you have ignored me. So maybe, just maybe, before it's too late, you will pay attention now." What a wake-up call. Is it scary? Of course it is. I have lost a cousin and a dear friend at the time of this writing. Yet, when I take a deep breath and remember that I am immersed in the love of family and friends, encased in the armor of my own power and wisdom, and guarded by my ancestors and my God, I relax. I AM!

Can we face COVID-19 and be victorious and come out on the other side of this disease? Yes. Do we have the tools to do so? Yes. We must pay attention to science. Will we be better for the journey? Absolutely. When all else fails, go back to Chapter 1. Celebrate New Beginnings.

We are a resilient species.

* *COVID-19 - See Glossary*

Elaine Robnett Moore

* Necklace - Zebras - Ceramic, Wood, Sterling, Rubber

78

Guardianship of Earth

Elaine Robnett Moore

> *"Planet Earth is our only home.*
> *We have an obligation to treasure, protect and*
> *preserve it in order for Earth to be able to sustain*
> *our children and all future generations."*
> -erm

Throughout these chapters, I have mentioned wonders I have experienced both in my neighborhood and as I have traveled. I have marveled at the beauty of places and images like sunsets on the South China Sea, beautiful rainbows (sometimes double), tree top bridges in Ghana, the hills of Kigali, Rwanda, the peaceful waters of the Caribbean Sea, cherry blossoms in Spring, orangutans on the island of Borneo, and so much more. While I have been amazed by these wonders, I know that, if these opportunities are to be available for our descendants, we are going to have to be far more proactive and persistent regarding conservation, restoration, and protection of this earth and all of its inhabitants. This includes wildlife in danger of extinction due to the reckless behavior of humans.

While this is not pleasant, let me be candid. Humans have managed to destroy, devastate and outright kill through pollution, greed and negligence. The severity of earthquakes, tsunamis, hurricanes, tornados, glaciers melting, global warming, and the senseless eradication of numerous species of animals, insects and plants, is a direct result of our negligence, greed and casual disregard for other species.

The wonder and beauty of this planet is fragile and in need of our immediate protection. Each of us is responsible for the welfare of this Earth. We must be active participants as guardians. We cannot ignore the need to replenish and reinvigorate life on this Earth. We have a role to play in adding to the continued perfection and energy of this planet. While we can enjoy its many wondrous gifts, we have an absolute responsibility to contribute in every way possible to the conservation, protection, and restoration of our natural environment and wildlife.

When you think of art and elevating spiritual awareness, you realize that nature is art in its purest form. Our spiritual journey is aided when we can see this art: an eagle (endangered) in flight, or a cheetah (endangered) in pursuit of its prey. Gone are the Javan, Caspian, and Bali tigers that once moved through jungles in all their majesty (all extinct within the last seventy years). It is remotely possible to see an Amur leopard (endangered) resting languidly in the sun (only thirty are known to be left). A hot button honey bee (soon to be added to the list of endangered species) darting from flower to flower, or thousands of acres of rainforest in South America teaming with plants and insects that hold the key to medicines that could protect us, are going and gone. These wonders that engage our every sense, and sustain our lives, are rapidly disappearing.

What is left for those coming after us is a colorless, disease ridden, bleak world. What will they have to build from? What will their dreams be? What can they hope for? What colors will brighten their thoughts? Will they have options? Clearly, the experiences we seek to have or leave for our descendants are already diminished considerably.

Our options are few. We can actively engage in the solutions that are already available to us. We can conserve energy, reuse, and participate in the preservation of wildlife. We can support maintaining or putting controls on companies polluting our environment, destroying our waterways, our air, and the ground we rely on. All of the above reinforces a healthy balance between nature and humankind. Every single step each of us takes toward replenishing our planet collectively ensures our ability to leave this earth a better place for our descendants.

We have an obligation to do this for our children, for future generations, as well as for our own peace of mind.

On guard.

Elaine Robnett Moore

* Mirror, Mirror -Mother of Pearl, Swarovski Crystal, Rubber

79

Kindness

Elaine Robnett Moore

> *"It is indeed the strongest fiber woven into the armor of our heroes. A random act of kindness is one the greatest gifts you can give."*
> *-erm*

What is kindness? It is the quality of being friendly, generous, and considerate. It is performing a selfless act. It is offering a service to someone with no expectation of receiving something in return. Sometimes it is a random act of kindness and sometimes it is a fearless act of kindness.

It is a sacrifice that brings joy, hugs, a smile, and sometimes, tears of gratitude. It may be a sacrifice of time, of goods, sometimes of safety, of family, of pain, and always more. It can be the giving of one's life to save others. It can be holding a door for someone.

How do these acts look?

- o A child sharing their candy
- o A first responder holding the hand of a dying patient
- o Caregivers who treat the elderly with dignity
- o People donating food, clothing, money to those in need
- o Someone who takes a friend to an appointment

- One who grocery shops for a shut-in
- The one who feeds your animal while you are away
- The grandparent who watches the baby so you get a night off
- A friend who calls to check on you
- A smile to a stranger
- A random hug
- An intuitive hug
-
-
-
-

Feel free to add your acts of kindness here.

There are heroic acts of kindness sprinkled throughout this book. Acts I have been the recipient of that have left me eternally grateful, like a hug shared over 45 years ago that still reminds me of what unconditional love really is. Find a way to share a hug, virtual or real, a thumbs up, a smile, a kind word, a meal, or a thank you, with someone everyday.

The staff at the Hebrew Home of Greater Washington, Wasserman Building 4 West, exhibited a great example of kindness. I am specifically grateful to those who have taken exceptional care of my aunt, *Mildred Franklin, for the last five years. They are the heroes that I am eternally indebted to. They have given her love, showered her with laughter, wrapped her in kindness, and hugged her in patience. They have always gone above and beyond their assigned duties to assure her well-being. By doing this for my aunt, they have demonstrated unbelievable kindness. May their lives be as full of love as the love they have

Elaine Robnett Moore

given her. Their kindness is the foundation upon which this world is built. They are the exemplification of kindness.

Share random acts of kindness.

* *Mildred P. Franklin - See Glossary*

Elaine Robnett Moore

* Necklace - Rain Forest - Emeralds, Chevrons, 22k Gold, Vermeil

80

I Am a Butterfly

Elaine Robnett Moore

"Butterflies are free."
-erm

I believe, as we grow in self-awareness, we morph into the beautiful creatures we are designed to be. In celebration of this transformation, I composed this poem. I hope that you see yourself as you read it.

I Am a Butterfly

I am
   A butterfly
My wings are
   Beautiful iridescent
Rainbows
   Ever changing
   Ever constant
Sprinkled with stardust
   To encourage
   Free flight
Elusive transparencies
Designed to
Absorb wisdom / joy / love
   Sweet tears / laughter
Designed to
   Repel ignorance / pain / hatred
     Blue times / indifference
My antennas are
   Long fine delicate
   Life feelers
     Reaching out
     Reaching in
   Dipped in dreams
     To know
     Reality
Touching tentacles
Sensitive to
   The breath of a

Elaine Robnett Moore

Newborn hummingbird
Sensitive to
The agony of
An unsung song
Music explodes
Wings unfold
I AM A BUTTERFLY

-Elaine Robnett Moore

Elaine Robnett Moore

* Elaine Robnett Moore wearing Shangri-La, ensemble from Pua Studio, photograph by Zarmina Said

81

Legacy

Elaine Robnett Moore

> *"Your light in my life continues to make it rich and full and wonderful."*
> *-erm*

The most important thing I know is that I am here because of each and every one of you. If you are meeting me on the pages of this book, please include yourselves. It is the cumulative love, laughter, tears, hugs, and energy of all of you through time that makes me who I am.

You have contributed to the molding of me into the Elaine Marie, Elaine, Lainie, Momma, Mommy, Mimi, Nana, Grandmother, Grandma, Auntie, Great Grandmother, little Elaine, Girlfriend, Sista, Miss Elaine, and Elaine Robnett Moore I am today. Loving you is one of my greatest joys. You keep me young in spirit, and engaged in life.

If you have passed me by,	*I'm coming.*
If you haven't caught up,	*Come on.*
If you wonder if you are worthy,	*Of course you are.*
I promise you life here is	*Absolutely, Spectacularly, Wonderfully Divine!*

Thank you for being a part of my life.

Elaine Robnett Moore

About the Author

Elaine Robnett Moore born April 7, 1944, is a fourth-generation, internationally renowned artist whose mediums of choice are beaded jewelry and the written word. She is a self-taught designer for thirty plus years. She finds inspiration in using beads, poetry, and conversations while teaching as a means of empowering women globally.

Raised in St. Louis, Missouri, and mother of five, Elaine's diverse background includes real estate sales, management and development, including Dawson Manor, a multi-unit housing complex built in southern Illinois, which in today's market would be equivalent to twenty one million dollars. She was the first African American to take a new commercial office building of seventy thousand plus square feet, from 0 to 70% occupancy in only two years. Her penchant for business development brought many entrepreneurs to her door seeking assistance and access to her extensive, domestic and international network.

As an international development consultant in Africa, the Caribbean, and Malaysia working with bead artists and artisans, she assisted an artist and women's co-op in Kigali, Rwanda, in creating a new bead now being marketed in the U.S. and Europe. She orchestrated the development of the first wholly Bahamian owned jewelry manufacturing business in the Bahamas and oversaw the development of the largest jewelry supply source in the Caribbean in Barbados, West Indies.

As her work and experience in these countries grew, so did her sensibilities around art and culture. From the synergy of her creativity and business acumen, she honed her art and the business, Elaine Robnett Moore Designs (previously known as Elaine Robnett Moore Collection) that developed around it.

Her work has been published and exhibited internationally. She was guest speaker at the International Bead & Beadwork Conference November 2007, in Istanbul, Turkey, where she presented a paper, "Messengers From The Past, Ambassadors to the Future". She was guest speaker at the conference in October 2015 in Kuching, Sarawak, Malaysia where she presented a paper, "The Art of Bead Stringing - Artist to Entrepreneur". She was invited, as a master teacher, to the Borneo International Bead Conference in 2017 and October of 2019.

She has served on the board of directors and as president of the Bead Society of Greater Washington, where she is still an active member. She served on the board of directors of the Bead Museum in Washington, D.C., until it closed in 2008. In April of 2016, she was appointed to the Board of Directors of the Arts and Humanities Council of Montgomery County.

In May of 2013, Elaine was commissioned by the government of Rwanda to write the first training manual, *Professional Jewellery Making with Beads*. It focused on how to design and produce beaded jewelry and how to then turn these skills into a business. The second edition of her book, *The Art of Bead Stringing Artist to Entrepreneur*, was published April 2015.

Glossary

Maya Angelou
Maya Angelou (April 4, 1928 - May 28, 2014) was an American poet, singer, memoirist, and civil rights activist, best known for her 1969 memoir, *I Know Why the Caged Bird Sings*.

Jabari Asim
Jabari Asim (August 11, 1962 -) is an American author, journalist, poet, playwright, associate professor of writing, literature and publishing at Emerson College, Boston, Massachusetts. Formerly an editor at the Washington Post, and Editor-in-Chief of the NAACP's The Crisis, he has written seventeen books, including fiction, nonfiction, and children's literature and co-wrote the book and lyrics for Brother Nat, a musical about Nat Turner's 1831 slave uprising.

Tom Bass
Tom Bass (January 5, 1859 - November 4, 1934) was an American Saddlebred horse trainer. Bass was born into slavery, but became one of the most popular horse trainers of the late nineteenth and early twentieth centuries. Bass trained the influential Saddlebred stallion Rex McDonald, as well as horses owned by Buffalo Bill Cody, Theodore Roosevelt, and Will Rogers.

Maida J. Coleman

Maida J. Coleman (1954 -) is a Missouri State Representative 2001, Missouri State Senator 2002 - 2009, and Commissioner for Missouri Public Service Commission 2015 to present.

COVID-19

COVID-19 is a mild to severe respiratory illness that is caused by a coronavirus (Severe acute respiratory syndrome coronavirus 2 of the genus Betacoronavirus), is transmitted chiefly by contact with infectious material (such as respiratory droplets), and is characterized especially by fever, cough, and shortness of breath, and may progress to pneumonia and respiratory failure —called also coronavirus disease 2019.

Alexandre Dumas

Alexandre Dumas - born Dumas Davy de la Pailleterie [dymɑ davi də la pajət(ə)ʁi]; 24 July 1802 – 5 December 1870),[1][2] also known as Alexandre Dumas père (where père is French for 'father', thus 'the elder/senior'), was a French writer. His works have been translated into many languages, and he is one of the most widely read French authors. Many of his historical novels of high adventure were originally published as serials, including *The Count of Monte Cristo, The Three Musketeers, Twenty Years After,* and *The Vicomte of Bragelonne: Ten Years Later.* His novels have been adapted since the early twentieth century into nearly 200 films. (see Wikipedia Alexandre Dumas).

Alexandre Dumas, *fils*

Alexandre Dumas *fils* ('son') - (1824–1895), son of Alexandre Dumas and also a novelist, author of *The Lady of the Camellias*, which has in turn become the source for many plays, operas, ballets.

George Perry Floyd Jr.

George Perry Floyd Jr. (October 14, 1973 - May 25, 2020) was an African American man, killed in Powderhorn, a neighborhood south of downtown Minneapolis, Minnesota. Derek Chauvin, a white police officer, knelt on Floyd's neck for almost eight minutes while Floyd, who was handcuffed and lying face down on the city street, begging for his life and could be heard repeatedly saying, "I can't breathe." After his death, protests against police violence toward black people quickly spread across the United States and internationally. Floyd grew up in Houston, Texas. wikipedia.org.

Mildred P. Franklin

Mildred P. Franklin (1921 -) is an artist, and a pianist who was once, as a teenager, invited to play with the St. Louis Symphony Orchestra. Later, she worked with Scott Joplin as his assistant, helping him compose music. She owned the first African American Dance Studio west of the Mississippi River. She taught ballet, tap, pointe and contemporary dance. She was taught by a European ballet master. In her earlier years, she taught typing at Sumner High School in St. Louis. Missouri.

Omi Gray

Omi Gray (May 19, 1950 -) is a multi-faceted teaching artist living in Harlem, New York. She specializes in jewelry fiber art.

Francois M. Guyol de Guiran

Francois M. Guyol de Guiran (1776 - 1849) was an artist, a French-émigré miniaturist, who came to America in the early nineteenth century, when the market was especially strong for such delicate likenesses. Guyol de Guiran worked in St. Louis (1812–ca. 1820) and in New Orleans (1822 - 1828); His Paintings are in the Metropolitan Museum of Art, New York and The St. Louis Art Museum, St. Louis, MO.

David F. James

David F. James (Nov. 17, 1923 - July 23, 2016) was an Army Air Corps officer and attorney. He was a Tuskegee Airman who from 1944 to 1945, flew combat missions with the 332nd Fighter Group over Germany, as well as other countries in Eastern Europe, during World War II. He went on to become an attorney accomplishing many 'firsts' as an African American during his illustrious career. See thehistorymakers.org and Wikipedia.

Bill Kohn

William Roth Kohn (1931 - 2004) was born, worked, and lived in St. Louis as a painter. He is celebrated for his use of vibrant color and dizzying perspectives in his paintings of significant places around the world. In his work, he illuminated the architecture and landscapes of places such as the Duomo in Florence, Machu Picchu in Peru, the bridges of Paris, and the Grand Canyon. Kohn exhibited across the United States as well as internationally in Japan, India, and Mexico. In addition to painting, Kohn had a forty-year teaching career at Washington University School of Art in St. Louis.

Shirley LeFlore
Shirley LeFlore (March 6, 1940 - May 12, 2019) was one of St. Louis, Missouri's, most influential performance art poets. She split her time between performances in New York City and teaching creative writing at the University of Missouri, St. Louis. One of the premiere women's voices in St. Louis, Shirley was a part of many underground activists poetry organizations.

Hannelore McDaniel
Hannelore McDaniel (1954 -) is a Harlem artist, born in Germany; she studied art in Cologne and New York. She is a jewelry designer specializing in beaded jewelry. Her background is as a collage and graphic artist.

Innocent Nkurunziza
Innocent Nkurunziza (1986 -) is one of the leading contemporary artists in Rwanda. He is a talented painter, sculptor, installation artist, bead maker, and jewelry designer. Along with his brother Emmanuel Nkuranga, he founded Inema Arts Center in 2012. As the leading source of

contemporary art in Rwanda, Inema Arts Center spurs creativity for personal, social and economic growth.

Joan Rosenstein and Ken Roberts
Joan Rosenstein and Ken Roberts (R&R Photography) is a husband and wife partnership, which has provided the Washington, D.C. Metro area with high quality, long lasting family photo restorations since 1992.

Zarmina Said
Zarmina Said (1953 -) is an artist, couturier, jewelry artist, potter, shoe designer, and founder of Pua Naturally a Washington, D.C. based, retail studio. She works directly with a cooperative of master tailors, seamstresses and block printers in Nepal and India.

Joyce J. Scott
Joyce J. Scott (1948 -) is an African American artist, sculptor, quilter, performance artist, installation artist, print-maker, jewelry artist, lecturer and educator. She is the recipient of many awards among which being named a MacArthur Fellow in 2016, and a Smithsonian Visionary Artist in 2019.

Clara Robnett Scranage
Clara Robnett Scranage (Sept. 28, 1928 - Oct. 27, 1982) graduated from St. Louis University having had a full scholarship. She was told she had to maintain a 4.0 grade point

average to receive the full scholarship. She did. She was one of the first African American female astrophysicists that worked for the Navy, NASA, and the Jet Propulsion Laboratory (JPL) during the space race. She worked on the Apollo, the space shuttle, and numerous satellites, winning an award for her work in Mars atmosphere and it's effect on space travel. She also worked on the MX missile but left her contracted job due to the conviction that she had that the multiple warheads on the missiles were immoral.

Breonna Taylor
Breonna Taylor (June 5, 1993 - March 13, 2020) was a twenty-six-year-old African American emergency medical technician, who was fatally shot by Louisville Metro Police Department (LMPD) officers on March 13, 2020. Three plainclothes LMPD officers executing a no-knock search warrant entered her apartment in Louisville, Kentucky. Gunfire was exchanged between Taylor's boyfriend Kenneth Walker and the officers. The officers were in the wrong apartment. wikipedia.org.

Vedanta
Vedanta is one of the six (āstika) schools of Hindu philosophy. Vedanta literally means "end of the Vedas", reflecting ideas that emerged from the speculations and philosophies contained in the Upanishads.

Wakanda

Wakanda is a fictional country appearing in American comic books published by Marvel Comics. It is located in Sub-Saharan Africa, and is home to the superhero Black Panther. Officially known as the Kingdom of Wakanda, it is a small fictional nation in North East Africa. In the story, for centuries they have remained in isolation and are now considered the most technologically advanced nation of the planet. Birnin Zana is the capital and largest city. Wakanda is part of the Black Panther (Marvel) story line.